"Greg Cochran is my friend and he w̶ ̶ ̶ ̶ ̶ ̶ ̶ ̶ ̶ ̶ ̶ ̶ has given more thought to the issue of the persecuted church than any other one hundred Christians I know combined. This book is a distillation of much of that thought. If you're skimming this endorsement to determine if you want to read the book, please allow me to offer a suggestion. Read the story of Sister Yuen in the Introduction. If that doesn't open your heart to be concerned about the issue discussed in this book then you should pray for the Lord to help you with your hardness of heart."

Donald S. Whitney, *Professor of Biblical Spirituality*
The Southern Baptist Theological Seminary
(www.biblicalspirituality.org)

"Finally, a book has been written to speak for those needing a voice in the American church. In this book, Greg Cochran has done a superb job of addressing Christian persecution throughout the world in a way that is clear, well-researched, biblically sound, and practically insightful. No one will be able to read this book and be unmoved by the author's powerful call to prioritize the persecuted for Christ around the world. Read this book! I dare you. Just know that you will not be the same after."

Brian Croft, *Senior Pastor, Auburndale Baptist Church*
Founder, Practical Shepherding (http://practicalshepherding.com/)
Senior Fellow, Church Revitalization Center,
The Southern Baptist Theological Seminary

"Persecution lies in the context of much of the Scriptures, and persecution emerges as a significant theme throughout the biblical story. Persecution also remains the daily reality for millions of Christians, and is in some sense the experience of all Christians. *Christians in the Crosshairs: Persecution in the Bible and around the World Today* sheds biblical, theological, missional, and practical light on this difficult but awe-inspiring theme of persecution. Clear, edifying, thoughtful, and mature, this book is based on years of research, teaching, pastoral ministry, and praying about persecution. Even more, it is important for understanding the Bible, persecution, the church, our mission, the culture, and ourselves."

Chris Morgan, *Dean and Professor of Theology*
California Baptist University

CHRISTIANS *in the* CROSSHAIRS

Persecution in the Bible and around the World Today

GREGORY C. COCHRAN

WEAVER BOOK
COMPANY
WOOSTER, OHIO

Cover: Frank Gutbrod
Interior design and typesetting: {In a Word}
Editing: Line for Line Publishing Services

Print: 978-1-941337-61-5
EPUB: 978-1-941337-62-2

Library of Congress Cataloging-in-Publication Data

Names: Cochran, Gregory C., 1966- author.
Title: Christians in the crosshairs : persecution in the Bible and around the world today /
    Gregory C. Cochran.
Description: First edition. | Wooster : Weaver Book Company, 2016.
Identifiers: LCCN 2016012928 | ISBN 9781941337615
Subjects: LCSH: Persecution—Biblical teaching. | Persecution.
Classification: LCC BR1601.3 .C675 2016 | DDC 272—dc23
LC record available at https://lccn.loc.gov/2016012928

Dedicated to my bride,
to my father's bride, and to the bride of Christ

CONTENTS

Contents

ACKNOWLEDGMENTS

No book gets published without untold hours of dedication both from the author and from the many others necessary to make the publication happen. In this process, I have come to appreciate greatly the work of Jim Weaver and Weaver Book Company. I am thankful for his desire to publish high-quality biblical literature for the local church. I am thankful for his recognizing the great need for ministry to those suffering persecution and for his willingness to bring this publication to fruition.

My own desire to understand persecution began many years ago in an unsuspecting way when I was confronted with a free newsletter from Voice of the Martyrs ministry. That encounter began a journey that has taken me from ministry opportunities to Ph.D. study. I am grateful that the Southern Baptist Theological Seminary accepted my dissertation proposal and allowed me to pursue this subject academically — at a time when few people were thinking about the study of persecution. I am particularly thankful for the helpful insights and the strong critique I received from Dr. Mark Seifrid, who served on my Ph.D. supervisory committee and greatly sharpened my understanding of persecution in the New Testament.

My colleagues at California Baptist University have also provided further sharpening through many conversations on the various aspects of persecution. Three colleagues in particular have been remarkably helpful to me. Tony Chute has an uncanny ability to deliver succinct, clever remarks that cause me often to rethink entire trains of thought. Thank you, Tony.

Likewise, Jeff Mooney, professor of Old Testament, has for many years helped me think through this topic. His insights on the obligation of Christians toward the covenant community are nothing short of brilliant. I am so thankful for his input.

Most of all, I am thankful for Chris Morgan, a dean who encourages thorough academic study while modeling the heart of a servant. Chris dedicated personal time to reading the manuscript and offering invaluable critiques, which have undoubtedly made this book much better than it would have been without his input. Whatever shortcomings still remain are completely my fault and likely exist because I failed to follow Dr. Morgan's wise advice.

Many friends have offered feedback on several of the chapters (thank you, Cesar and Rachel Solis). Other friends, like Jen Yakel and Steven Pugh, have offered prayers and encouragement through the long struggle. My family has been supportive of this task in many ways. My children have handled chores around the home to make writing and editing possible. They have read and offered feedback on the chapters as well. I am so thankful that God has blessed me with children who are moving into adulthood with faith in our Lord Jesus Christ.

Of all the support and encouragement I've received, none has surpassed what my wife has offered. Vickie is an excellent book editor. She has critiqued and edited countless pages of my writing over the years. If the book is clear and readable, then you, too, can thank Vickie. She is greater than any wife I could have imagined for myself. God has blessed me beyond measure in giving me a bride who delights in holiness and excellence for his name's sake.

My hope for all who read this volume is a strengthened faith. One of the most surprising aspects of studying persecution has been its effect on me. I thought it would be dour and woeful and defeating. But the opposite was true. This is because the gospel — with its resurrection power — is able to take the worst situations and reframe them in victory. Hearing stories of triumph through suffering has been nothing short of glorious. Studying persecution biblically has led to the same conclusion. The gospel is truly the power of God to salvation for all who believe (Rom. 1:16). Studying persecution has encouraged stronger faith. My hope is that this book will have such an effect on you as you consider what the Scriptures teach about persecution.

INTRODUCTION:

WHY THIS BOOK ON CHRISTIAN PERSECUTION?

> *Indeed, all who desire to live godly in Christ Jesus will be persecuted.*
>
> *(2 Tim. 3:12)*

She had not sung a solo on our stage before, but little Anna Grace — with her beautiful red hair and her round blue eyes sparkling more brightly than any Christmas lights ever could — offered a stirring performance of "Little Lamb," which left the audience overjoyed, actually needing to applaud just to have a form of release for its delight. Anna Grace was adorable. Her cuteness alone merited applause, yet, for her, the song was clearly neither about herself nor for the audience. Her audience was one: her dad.

Her dad was playing guitar next to her as she sang. As soon as the song was complete (and the applause erupted), Anna Grace's arms were extended — but not to her adoring fans. Rather, her hands reached for her father and hugged him ever so tightly, as if to say, "Did you like that, Daddy? I did it for you." Anna Grace was delighted to have offered her best performance for her father. Her reward was far greater than the audience's approval: she received the delighted embrace of her father's love. The audience merely served as witness to the spectacle of this event.

The Christian life is supposed to be like this loving embrace. As Paul says, we offer our lives as living sacrifices, holy and acceptable to God, which is our worship (Rom. 12:1). Like Anna Grace, we seek to please our Father who is in heaven. We offer service to the church and service to the world, hoping above all else to please our heavenly Father — not so we can hear the enthusiastic outbursts of admiring fans, but so we can hear the single most-glorious statement of our delight: "Well done, good and faithful servant" (Matt. 25:23).

As faithful Christ-followers in America, we are blessed with an abundance of instructors, pastors, and teachers who can help us run the race that is set before us (Heb. 12:1). We aren't yet perfect, but we are well supplied with Bibles and sermons. We aren't giving up. We desire to live a godly life in Christ Jesus. Now, it is time for us to face the facts about what such a desire means.

This desire means that we *are* Christian, and the more we grow in our Christ-likeness, the more we become peculiar to the world. The more we aim to please our Father in heaven, the more we may displease the world around us. Everyone can recognize the sweetness of a child seeking to please her father, but rarer is the unbeliever who can admit the goodness of a child of God seeking to please his heavenly Father — especially when pleasing the Father might mean speaking against the status quo of sexual preferences in the aftermath of the sexual revolution. Therefore, the Bible promises *all* Christian believers — even those in the United States — that we will be persecuted. As Paul says, "Indeed, all who desire to live godly in Christ Jesus will be persecuted" (2 Tim. 3:12).

The book you are reading is my own attempt to understand the declaration of 2 Timothy 3:12 in light of the entire biblical teaching about Christian persecution. Inevitably, this perspective expects a peculiarity about the Christian that is not shared by the majority of people in the world. The Christian is one who has been rescued out of the domain of darkness and transferred to the kingdom of God's only begotten Son (Col. 1:13). Christians are a peculiar people because they are a chosen race, a royal priesthood, a holy nation, aliens and strangers to the world (1 Peter 2:9–10). Christians, though in the world, are not of the world (John 17:14–18). According to James (the brother of Jesus), Christians must be careful not to be friends with the world, for the one who makes himself a friend of the world makes himself an enemy of God (James 4:4). Understanding the exact nature of the enmity between the world and the Christian is critical for understanding Christian persecution.

I have a conviction that there is much left unsaid to the Christian worshiping on Sunday in America. For some reason, pastors and church leaders are oftentimes uncomfortably silent on the issue of persecution. From personal experience, I have seen a reticence among pastors, professors, and publishers when it comes to speaking out or trying to understand Christian persecution. Nevertheless, I think persecution is on the minds of more Christians than church leaders recognize. My hope is that this book will do more than strengthen and encourage my fellow Christians; my hope is that it will also awaken Christian leaders to the reality of Christian persecution in the here and now.

Even when persecution is addressed, those speaking of it tend to do so as though it is something still to come — a sinister villain crouching like a predator, hiding over the horizon, and waiting to pounce on the church at the onset of a future millennium. Or, perhaps worse, persecution is wielded like a club by some preachers to demand adherence to a pretribulation rapture so the Christian can believe he will be spared from its severity. Such thinking may be the product of an over-indulgent American prosperity. Christians in most of the world already suffer severely on account of their allegiance to Christ.

I remember a conversation with a Christian friend whose main argument for a pretribulation rapture was that it would make sure the church didn't have to go through such an awful time of suffering. Forgetting for a moment the reality that persecution tends to empower rather than to diminish the church, this idea of presenting persecution as though it can be avoided by a future rapture is far off the biblical mark. Christians are presently going through intense persecution in more than three dozen countries around the world.

Imagine saying to Sister Yuen of Shanghai that she won't have to face persecution because there will be a future rapture of the church. Sister Yuen is a Christian widow with two children who were quite young when she was arrested by Communists in China for her faith. Her mother took care of the children while Yuen was in prison — until Yuen's mother died. The Communists then said they would show compassion to Yuen, telling her to pack her bags and get ready to go home to care for her little ones. Excitedly, she packed her bags and hurriedly entered the room to see her two precious children. Once in the room with her children, Sister Yuen was told that she was free to leave with her babies — as soon as she signed a note renouncing Christ. The guard asked her what she wanted: Jesus or her children. Her children's brown eyes filled with tears as they cried, "Mummy, we miss you! Please come home!"[1] Would she forsake Christ — or her little ones? Sister Yuen could not deny the Lord who bought her, and her children were taken away from her. They were told that she didn't care for them.

After this brief encounter with her children, Sister Yuen was forced to stay in a Communist prison for the next twenty-three years — more than eight thousand days — without them. Could you imagine a more tortuous bondage for a mother on this earth? There is no doubt Sister Yuen faced decades of mental and physical torture from this evil perpetrated against her on account of her faith in Christ. She immediately pursued her son when she was released. He rejected her, telling her that he had no mother. He rejected Christ, too, because he believed Christ robbed him of his mother (see Luke 12:53).

Sister Yuen is not a believer from long ago. Her story is fresh, and it is real today in China. Speaking of persecution as though it is yet on the horizon is somewhat akin to a carpenter who strikes his nails on the left or the right side of their heads. Though his hammer strikes a blow, his work is counter-productive. His nails become bent rather than driven usefully into the wood. The result is frustration rather than a solid structure. Indeed, more work is created in that the nails must be removed or at least straightened before the building efforts can resume. Similarly, our conversations concerning perse-cution — when they do happen — are often off just a bit to the left or to the right of the nail heads themselves, leaving us in a position of needing a more solid structure for understanding persecution.

Whereas some would have Christians put the context of persecution into the distant future, others see persecution only in the distant past. They speak of persecution as though it happened only in the Coliseum in Rome, in the days of Caesars, lions, and gladiators. But Christian persecution did not end when the Christian Constantine became the emperor of the Roman Empire. Persecution continued through the Dark Ages and flared up again throughout the Protestant Reformation. Persecution in fact has never ceased. It is still with us today and will remain until the return of Christ. As a Voice

---

1   Brother Yun et al., *Back to Jerusalem: Three Chinese House Church Leaders Share Their Vision to Complete the Great Commission* (Waynesboro, GA: Piquant, 2003), 118. This story of Sister Yuen is adapted from this book.

of the Martyrs T-shirt rightly reminds us, "Persecution did not end at the Coliseum." One need neither to travel back in time nor to project himself into the future to find it because persecution is reality for millions of Christians around the world every day for all to see (i.e., those whose eyes are not blinded by the god of this world [2 Cor. 4:4]).

Still others speak of persecution as though it were something to expect "over there" in Muslim countries or Communist countries, but not in Europe or America. Such talk, again, proves to be both unwise and unwarranted. After all, the Word of God is still binding, right? Christians claim the covenant promises of God for themselves. Whether 2 Timothy 3:12 is a Bible promise is debated, but regardless of whether one calls it a promise or a declaration, the statement makes clear that Christians can expect to suffer persecution: "Indeed, all who desire to live godly in Christ Jesus will be persecuted."

Persecution does happen in Muslim nations and Communist countries (and Hindu and Buddhist enclaves), but it is not unique to those places of the world. The declaration of 2 Timothy 3:12 is a word to *all* Christians who desire godliness in Christ — not just a word to Christians who desire Christ in Muslim contexts. All Christians who desire godliness in Christ will be persecuted. This is a clear statement from God. If we take this statement as a promise, then the promise would be akin to the one found in Hebrews 12:7, which promises discipline for every true child of God. These two promises might well be the two greatest promises of God that nobody seems to want, but they remain priceless encouragements that God is ever faithful and ever present with his people. Persecution is assured for the believer.

Christians need to speak more often — and more clearly — about persecution. This book attempts to do just that. It explains what the Bible teaches about the dynamic of Christian persecution — to understand the topic in the here and now. My hope is to provide a structure that will lead Christians to a Christ-glorifying response to their persecution, while clarifying why all Christians — even those of us in America — should be (and in fact probably are being) persecuted.

It may sound strange to speak of Christians in America being persecuted, but — as you will learn through the discussions in this book — persecution is an inseparable part of the Christian faith. The fact that I have never been thrown into prison on account of Christ is a lack of degree of persecution, not a lack of kind. Later chapters explain this more fully. Suffice it to say for now that Jesus defines persecution in Matthew 5:10–12 in such a way that it includes insults, slanders, and falsehoods. Any Christian who has not felt the brunt of insults and slanders has not been much of a witness for Christ. Testify for Christ in word and in deeds, and you will hear the insults and mocking, even as Christ himself heard such tauntings on the hill called Calvary.

Even more to the point, Christians are targets for persecution in America, but violence against Christians is not publicized the way violence against other groups is heralded. For example, a recent *Christianity Today* article noted that in 2012 alone, there were 115 shootings at churches across the country; 63 of those shootings led to fatalities.[2] And in 2015, 9 Christians were shot and killed at a Wednesday night prayer service at the Charleston AME (African Methodist Episcopal) church in South Carolina. To be sure, that shooting had an ugly racial element intertwined with it, but the shooter intentionally targeted these Christian churchgoers.

The truth of the matter is that all Christians are subject to persecution. Therefore, even experientially, all Christians ought to feel free to discuss persecution. Sure, some Christians face severe persecution of the more fantastic variety, including beatings, tortures, prison, and execution. They are to be especially revered for their faithful responses. We have much to learn from them.

However, they are not all that far removed from us since all of us are in the body of Christ (Heb. 13:3).[3] Christians should not separate themselves from the persecuted church. Persecution, according to the New Testament, belongs to all Christians *now*. Every child of God who — like Anna Grace — wants to please her Father will suffer some form of ridicule, slander, or suffering. Therefore, this volume aims to help all Christians understand the nature of Christian persecution.

Here's how the book is organized. Part 1 (chapters 1 and 2) seeks to define *Christian* persecution and explore where Christians are suffering around the

---

2 Melissa Steffan, "Church Shootings Prompt Pastors to Reevaluate Security," *Christianity Today*, accessed June 18, 2015, http://www.christianitytoday.com/gleanings/2012/november/church-shootings-prompt-pastors-to-reevaluate-security.html.

3 Most New Testament scholars insist that Hebrews 13:3 cannot refer to being in the body of Christ; rather, they understand the verse to mean "being in a body like them." For reasons that will be detailed in later chapters, I think it is appropriate to understand Hebrews 13:3 as meaning "in the body of Christ."

world. Part 2 (chapters 3–10) explores the Bible's teaching about persecution. Each of these chapters explains a specific book or portion of Scripture. For instance, the Gospels of Matthew and Mark are treated independently, while John is combined with Revelation, and Luke is combined with Acts. Several of Paul's letters are combined. Hebrews has a chapter of its own, and the two letters of Peter are considered together.

Part 3 (chapters 11–13) explains the implications of understanding persecution from a biblical and theological perspective. Chapter 11 looks at how Christ's presence is both the source *and* comfort of persecution. Chapter 12 explores why the church should make persecution a priority. And the concluding chapter summarizes the ground covered in the book and offers practical steps for making a difference.

PART 1

THE MEANING AND MAGNITUDE
OF CHRISTIAN PERSECUTION

1

TOWARD A DEFINITION

OF CHRISTIAN PERSECUTION AND MARTYRDOM

A man's enemies will be the members of his household.
(Matt. 10:36)

W hat do we mean when we say that Christians everywhere will suffer persecution? In Kentucky, a high school baseball player was dismissed from his team for missing practices on Sundays. Was he persecuted for being a Christian? In war-torn Sudan, Muslims from the north razed villages where Christians and animists once lived. Were those Christians suffering persecution? In Detroit, a group of street preachers were struck with rocks and bottles and harassed by police while trying to witness at a Muslim event. Were they persecuted? Christian lawyers like Gao Zhisheng fighting against the abuse of human rights in China have been imprisoned and tortured. Should their suffering be termed "persecution"?

Tryon Edwards, a great-grandson of Jonathan Edwards, once asserted, "Most controversies would soon be ended, if those engaged in them would first accurately define their terms, and then adhere to their definitions."[1] Edwards might have been too optimistic about the end of controversy, but he was right to note the power that definitions have to diffuse it. A trip to the local library or bookstore proves our faith in the power of definitions.

---

1 Tryon Edwards, ed., *A Dictionary of Thoughts: Being a Cyclopedia of Laconic Quotations from the Best Authors of the World, Both Ancient and Modern* (Detroit: F. B. Dickerson, 1914), 88.

The Power of Definitions

Consider the prevalence of English dictionaries. My local bookstore sells dictionaries for synonyms, war terms, business terms, legal terms, theological terms, and psychological terms. An almost endless stream of dictionaries flows out of an ocean of words. These words break upon the pages of our literature and land upon our minds, empowering creative thinking. Our thoughts actually ride upon a surf of words.

But words — like waves — do not always come as docile tides rolling in on a white sand shore. Rather, words break upon our ears and crash into our minds, often provoking crises. As the existentialist philosopher Jean-Paul Sartre once declared, "Words are loaded pistols."[2] Defining words, then, can be a dangerous game. Words are, in fact, the means by which reality takes (and keeps) its shape. Consider, for example, how the Nazis defined "treason" and "loyalty" for Germans in the 1940s — and consider the implications for Germany and the world!

In our own history, the word "person" has suffered terrible damage. In the nineteenth century, the word excluded a race of human beings who were subsequently bought and sold as slaves; those humans suffered the excruciating consequences of a horrible definition. Today, the word "person" excludes human babies developing in the womb, and the result causes untold pain and suffering for men and women in the aftermath of abortions — not to mention the millions of deaths of unborn babies. Subtle changes in the definitions of words can have cataclysmic long-term effects for us because definitions are significant.

Here we return to Edwards's point. Definitions do provide clarity and can lead to unity, but that unity does not always equate with what is good. Germany in 1942 and the South in 1840 were, for the most part, united in their definitions of key terms. (Thankfully, both of those thought-systems were eventually overthrown.) Here is why I said that Edwards was too optimistic about definitions ending controversy. Definitions of "treason" were clear in Nazi Germany. The definitions of words like "slave" and "free" were clear in the South. And war was the necessary outcome in each case. Often, clear definitions fuel controversy. Consider the definition of marriage.

---

2   Jean-Paul Sartre, *What Is Literature?* (New York: Harper & Row, 1965), 18.

The generally accepted evangelical definition of "marriage" — one man with one woman for a lifetime — is both perfectly clear and undeniably controversial. Paul Nyquist warns Christians concerning the new definition of marriage, saying, "It's impossible to overstate the impact of the abandonment of biblical marriage."[3] Nyquist's point is that the convenience of Christian living in America has been lost. If Nyquist is correct, then Christians must become ever more familiar with definitions of two key terms: "persecution" and "marriage."

Christians must define these two words clearly, as the two appear destined to remain hitched for decades. The term "marriage" is obviously undergoing a redefinition in our culture. The Defense of Marriage Act (DOMA) has fallen on notoriously difficult times. After the U.S. Supreme Court ruled in favor of recognizing gay marriage in the *Obergfell v. Hodges* decision, same-sex unions became legal in all fifty states. What the limits are to the new definition of marriage, no one knows. After a federal judge overturned Utah's ban of polygamous marriages, the 10th Circuit Court of Appeals in Denver is now deciding the famous "Sister Wives" case which condones group marriage.[4] In other states, relatives are seeking to define marriage as consenting adults — demanding freedom from the former restraint against incestuous relationships.

Because marriage is now redefined, Christians will be tested on whether we believe our own definitions. Do we as Christians believe God's monogamous design for heterosexual marriage? Will Christians stand on these convictions? What if group marriages, gay marriages, or even bestial marriages become matters of civil rights? Will Christians remain steadfast in their biblical convictions? Will we pay the price in persecution? What if a church loses its tax-exempt status as a result of monogamous marriage commitments? What if pastors are convicted of civil rights crimes — or hate crimes — and sent to jail for refusing to marry a small group of lovers?

Persecution may flow freely from the deluge of court decisions against traditional marriage. Already, Christian businesses have been shuttered for refusing to participate in gay wedding ceremonies. Surely, Christian churches

---

3   Paul Nyquist, *Prepare: Living Your Faith in an Increasingly Hostile Culture* (Chicago: Moody, 2015), 24.

4   This legal case involves Kody Brown and his four wives who are featured in the reality TV show called "Sister Wives," which airs on TLC.

and ministries will soon be in jeopardy.[5] Thus, Christians need adequate definitions of "marriage" and "persecution" so that we can understand what and why we are suffering — and have the right attitude and the right response to our suffering. We must, however, be careful with our definitions.

Returning to Sartre's point — that words are loaded pistols — we must think through the consequences of how we use the term "persecution." The definition we offer will shape Christian values and Christian practice. Those who suffer persecution are highly esteemed by the church — as they should be. In the spirit of Paul's admonition to imitate him the way he imitates Christ (2 Cor. 4:11), Christians have sought to imitate (and sometimes even venerate in an almost worshipful manner) those martyred for the faith. Christians watch and mimic the manners in which other Christians face persecution. Why? One reason is so they might imitate them in the way that Stephen, the first martyr after Christ, imitated his Lord through persecution. Christian moral character is shaped by how we define words like "persecution" and "martyr." As Christians, we need to know how to identify those among us who truly suffer persecution.

But here's the problem: persecution means many things to many different people. One recent article stated that wild birds were being persecuted in northern England.[6] Whatever the journalist covering bird crime in Great Britain meant by his use of the term, the Christian surely must understand it in a radically different way. Both Christians and birds of prey can be hunted and even threatened with extinction. Both Christians and wild birds can also give glory to God, but Christians alone are victimized explicitly on account of witnessing to their Creator's glory. Persecuting birds is not the same as persecuting Christians.

So, in the midst of our cultural confusion about marriage and with a dizzying array of popular definitions of persecution — covering everything from the birds of Great Britain to suicide bombers in the Middle East — Christians need clarity. What do we mean when we speak about Christian persecution today? A small controversy has erupted among theologians and missiologists attempting to answer this question.

---

5   See Jeff Iorg, ed., *Ministry in the New Marriage Culture* (Nashville: B & H Publishing Group, 2015).

6   See "Bird of Prey Persecution," published by the Royal Society for the Protection of Birds, accessed [on-line] March 8, 2016, at https://www.rspb.org.uk/forprofessionals/policy/wildbirdslaw/wildbirdcrime/birdsofprey/ .

Who Are the Persecuted?

Christians are not in agreement on the number of believers suffering persecution around the world. One recent news article reported that as many as 10 million Christians suffer persecution each year. While 10 million is a large number, it is a significantly small percentage of the more than 2 billion people on earth who claim to be Christians. Considering that the apostle Paul promised persecution to all who desire to live a godly life in Christ Jesus (2 Tim. 3:12), shouldn't the number be greater? Whether great or small, the number is difficult to pinpoint.

In the summer of 2013, *Christianity Today* published an article explaining why Christians have difficulty tallying numbers for persecution and martyrdom.[7] Groups like the Center for the Study of Global Christianity report that there are more than 100,000 martyrdoms per year,[8] while other groups such as Open Doors claim a more modest 1,200 martyrs per year. The problem is obvious. One figure puts the number of martyrs 83 times greater than the other. Why can't we agree on such a significant matter of Christian interest? The problem isn't with our math as much as it is with our definitions. Our lack of specificity is rooted in our lack of clearly defined terms. Until we can define "martyr" adequately, we cannot hope to count the number of martyrs accurately.

Christian leaders have been pleading for better definitions of "persecution" and "martyrdom" for decades. In 1974, the International Congress for World Evangelization (the Lausanne Congress) met to strategize the fulfillment of Christ's commission in Matthew 28:18–20. The Lausanne Congress was sober-minded enough to recognize that making disciples among all tribes and nations would lead to an increase in persecution: not all authorities are fond of Christianity! Thus, Lausanne called for increased study in the areas of Christian suffering — particularly in understanding what it means to

---

7   Sarah Eekhoff Zylstra, "Counting the Cost (Accurately): Why Tallies of Christian Martyrs Vary so Widely," *Christianity Today*, accessed February 15, 2015, http://www.christianity today.com/ct/2013/september/counting-cost-accurately.html.

8   See Todd M. Johnson, "The Case for Higher Numbers of Christian Martyrs," Center for the Study of Global Christianity, accessed April 5, 2015, http://www.gordonconwell.edu/ resources/documents/1martyrmethodology.pdf. Johnson argues for higher numbers and a broader definition to reflect the less technical definitions used by other religions (Judaism, Islam) for demographic purposes.

suffer *for Christ's sake*. Some thirty years later, in 2004, the Lausanne Congress published as a follow-up an occasional paper titled "The Persecuted Church," which reiterated, "There is clearly a need for deeper theological reflection on the issues pertaining to suffering, persecution, martyrdom, religious freedom, and human rights, and an appropriate Christian response."[9]

Now, more than ten years beyond Lausanne's occasional paper, the need for definition is only more acute. In reference to the wildly disparate numbers relating to martyrdom, the *Christianity Today* article notes, "Much of the discrepancy hinges on how researchers define martyr, and how closely they double-check each death."[10] Obviously, the first aspect of this diagnosis relates to the difficulty of defining "persecution" and "martyrdom," but even the second aspect depends on the very same thing. What would be the purpose of double-checking each death if it were not to discover whether the victim was actually a martyr? And how is one to determine whether a victim should be called a martyr without first understanding whether that person suffered persecution on account of Christ? It seems mandatory to build the definition of "martyr" on the logically prior foundation of the meaning of "persecution."

Researchers have been plagued by the question of whether or not a Christian's death was martyrdom. But to answer that question sufficiently, we must know if this person was persecuted on account of Christ. Instead of asking, "Did she die a martyr's death?" we should ask, "Was it persecution for Christ's sake that led to her death?" There is a degree of specificity that exists in the latter question; yet such a question still depends on our ability to define "persecution on account of Christ" sufficiently.

Toward a Definition

So, what is persecution on account of Christ? Nik Ripken's succinct definition gets right to the point: Christian persecution is "a negative reaction to

---

9   Patrick Sookhdeo, "The Persecuted Church," paper (no. 32) prepared for the Lausanne Committee for World Evangelization, Pattaya, Thailand, October 2004, accessed February 15, 2015, http://www.lausanne.org/wp-content/uploads/2007/06/LOP32_IG3.pdf.

10   Zylstra, "Counting the Cost."

the incarnate presence of Jesus."[11] Later chapters in this book put more flesh on this barebones definition. Already, this simple definition helps because it separates persecution from many other forms of suffering.

Consider the kinds of suffering persecution is not.[12] Human beings suffer for many reasons. Because we are in the world, we as Christians suffer as the rest of the world suffers. In 1976, an earthquake struck China and killed more than 250,000 people, including atheists, Buddhists, Muslims, and Christians. The so-called Christmas Tsunami of 2004 killed in excess of 280,000 people of varying faiths along the coast of Indonesia. And even in America, when heart disease strikes one of the 600,000 who will die from it this year, it will not first determine whether its victim is Christian. Christians, like all human beings, suffer from the frailties of the human condition: famine, disease, droughts, floods, and war.

None of this suffering is rightly called persecution. When we speak of *Christian* persecution, we are moving beyond suffering *as* Christians to a very specific form of suffering — suffering *because* we are Christian. Ripken's definition makes that plain. Christian suffering is persecution only when it occurs because of the presence of Jesus Christ.

Christians suffer two kinds of persecution: *individual* and *institutional*. Individual persecution occurs when a person acts alone against a Christian. Most often, this persecution will follow a witnessing encounter. In Boynton Beach, Florida, for instance, three former gangbangers went out on the street to tell others about the power of the gospel, which had converted them. These three street preachers connected with a young man named Jeriah Woody. For fifteen to twenty minutes, they shared the gospel with Woody and even spent a few minutes praying with him. As Woody parted ways with them, the three preachers continued seeking others to evangelize. But Woody abruptly returned and opened fire on the three men. One of the men escaped, but Stephen Ocean and Tite Sufra both died in the street on which

---

11   Nik Ripken, *The Insanity of Obedience: Walking with Jesus in Tough Places* (Nashville: B & H Publishing Group, 2014), 38.

12   The remainder of this book explores this definition in much more detail, adding nuances to it where appropriate. This definition reflects an Augustinian, Western tradition that includes the Roman Catholic notion of *in odium fidei*, which is persecution in hatred of the faith. However, biblically, the definition should rightly be anchored in Christ, rather than in faith or tradition.

they had been preaching. Woody acted alone, coldly murdering two street preachers in Florida after a witnessing encounter. This was an individual persecuting Christians.[13]

The second kind of persecution is *institutional*. Institutional persecution happens when organizations or government agencies exercise a strategy against Christianity in general or against particular followers of Christ. A classic twentieth-century example of institutional persecution was the persecution of confessing Christian pastors in Nazi Germany. The first Christian in Nazi Germany to suffer persecution unto death was Pastor Paul Schneider, who died at Buchenwald concentration camp after refusing to submit to the Nazi government's order forbidding him from preaching at his pulpit in Dickenshied. Police officers, prison guards, and Hitler Youth leaders were all part of a system that persecuted Schneider. His persecution was institutional.

These two kinds of persecution — institutional and individual — establish the general framework for understanding the kind of persecution most Christians suffer. The categories won't always be perfect, of course. Consider the case of Rifqa Bary, a teenager who fled her Ohio home and escaped to Florida after converting to Christ. According to Bary, she was afraid of her father carrying out an "honor killing" on account of her conversion from Islam to Christianity. The entire ordeal was highly publicized and went through several rounds of court trials. Though Bary did go back to Ohio, she never returned to her parents. Instead, she waited until she turned 18, filed for permanent resident status, and entered an American university. Was hers a case of individual persecution? Her father was reportedly the source of hostility. Or, was this institutional persecution, considering that her family was arrayed against her? Categorical lines are sometimes blurry. Institutions can stand behind an individual's persecuting actions just as institutional persecution is almost always carried out by a zealous individual.

While persecution occurs in only two *kinds*, it may take many *forms*. The most prevalent forms are categorized under the following headings: bias, slander, discrimination, incarceration, violence, and oppression. These forms of persecution can be carried out by either individuals or institutions.

---

13 While some have claimed that Woody's actions had nothing to do with this preaching encounter, the preaching event cannot be ignored as the immediate circumstance leading to Sufra and Ocean being killed. I consider further in this book what role the motive of the perpetrator has in determining whether an act is persecution.

For example, bias happens at the individual level when a person unwittingly avoids interaction with his Christian neighbor. Institutional bias might have occurred when news editors chose not to report on the case of Rifqa Bary, but to cover instead gay marriage or stories as ludicrous as Levi Johnston's plans to pose for *Playgirl* magazine. Media bias, after all, is most pernicious at the editorial level, where important news is often left unsaid. Bias goes unstated and even unnoticed. Thus, while it can be a form of persecution, bias is difficult to quantify. If a small business owner doesn't want to hire a particular Christian it might be because of his bias against Christians, but it could also be because he is biased against this particular Christian for another reason, such as his political party affiliation or his position on a certain social issue. Or the owner may not like the way the candidate is dressed. Perhaps the owner simply likes another candidate better. Bias is latent, under the surface, and not always easy to discern.

Slander, on the other hand, is malicious in a way that bias is not. Slander is always intentional, and it intends to harm — even if it must grossly distort the truth to do so. Jesus warned his followers (Matt. 5:10–12) that others would slander them on account of him. Most likely, Jesus was warning of the slander hurled at the disciples by Jewish leaders; if so, this would be a case of institutional slander. When one of the thieves on the cross slanderously asked Jesus why he couldn't deliver himself (and the two criminals) from crucifixion, he was acting alone. His was a case of individual slander. Slander does its damage against others by mocking, deriding, or diminishing their worth, reputation, or character.

Unlike slander, discrimination is a more tangible attempt to deprive someone of material goods or to hinder another person's overall well-being. A professor at Florida Atlantic University appears guilty of individual discrimination when he demanded that a Christian student write the name of Jesus on a paper and then place the paper on the ground and stomp on it. When the student refused to do so, the professor initiated discipline proceedings against him, depriving him of course credit toward degree completion. Eventually, a vice president for the school issued an apology on behalf of the professor and no further action was taken against the Christian student. If school administrators had joined in this discriminatory practice, then the episode would rightly have been called institutional discrimination. However, this discrimination seems to have been isolated to the one professor at the school.

The Shawano school district in Wisconsin, however, appears guilty of institutional discrimination in the case of Brandon Wegner. Wegner, who was 15 at the time, was asked by a teacher to write a "point-counterpoint" editorial opposing gay adoptions. He did, and he was disciplined for it by the teacher, who had asked him to write the editorial. In fact, Wegner's case reached the district superintendent, who allegedly berated the student, calling him ignorant and threatening him with suspension on account of his biblical opposition to homosexuality in general and gay adoption in particular. Eventually, the Liberty Counsel took action on behalf of Wegner and threatened the school district with legal action if he suffered any further repercussions. Neither the teacher nor anyone else showed concern about or made disparaging remarks toward the student who wrote the pro-gay adoption editorial. Wegner's view alone — based on his Christian faith — was confronted and belittled. At one point, the school district appeared ready to take away Brandon's status as a student. This is clearly discrimination based on his voicing Christian convictions.

Thus far, the forms of persecution we have discussed — bias, slander, and discrimination — are nonviolent. However, Christian persecution often occurs in violent forms. One form is incarceration. Incarceration is most often institutional — as most jails and prisons are operated by governments. It is not out of the question that individuals might kidnap or hold Christians as prisoners against their will through force or manipulation. Typically, however, rulers and institutions carry out incarcerations. Think here of the persecuting spirit of Saul of Tarsus before his conversion. In Acts 22, Paul offers his conversion testimony to fellow Jews, reminding them that he once opposed Christians so zealously that he cast believers into prison — both men and women (vv. 4–5). What was their crime? The crime was belonging to "the Way" (v. 4).

Though Paul would later mourn his actions, saying that he was unfit to be called an apostle because of his persecuting the church of God (1 Cor. 15:9), still he did not act on his own authority. He had received letters from the high priest and, effectively, represented the Judaism of his day (Acts 9:1–2). His was a case of institutional persecution, even though he individually was breathing threats and murders against Christians. Today, from China to Eritrea, from Uzbekistan to Egypt, Christians are still suffering in prisons as the victims of institutional persecution.

Beyond the physical restraint of incarceration, more violent forms of persecution abound. Christians in North Korea, for example, have suffered terrible violence under Communist dictatorships. In fact, few Christians remain in that dark place. In 1996, army officers discovered a Bible in an abandoned house near Nampo in North Korea. The Bible had a small piece of paper with the names of pastors and church members tucked into it. The army officers tracked down the twenty-five Christians named on the list and subsequently killed the five leaders in front of the other twenty church members. These five leaders were made to lie on the ground while a steamroller drove over their bodies, crushing them to death. After witnessing the gruesome execution of their Christian leaders, the other twenty Christians were led away to a labor camp.[14] Clearly, these Christians died from institutional, violent persecution perpetrated against them by an army unit in North Korea. Countless examples of individual violence against Christians are readily available. From a 10-year-old boy being thrown into a fire to a formerly Muslim woman having acid thrown onto her face to cause disfiguration, Christians suffer violence around the world on account of Christ. Just as Christ's physical body was beaten, scourged, and pierced while he was on the earth, so, now, the body of Christ still bleeds from the violence of persecution.

North Korea — because of the intense violence and massive incarcerations — has become an unfortunate example of the form of persecution called oppression. Oppression is a consummating form of persecution. When bias, discrimination, incarceration, and violence have done their work effectively, oppression ensues. Christians in North Korea — the few who are there — are oppressed. They are impoverished. They must hide their identity. They are not free. Their context itself attempts to suffocate the Christian life from them.

Christians are not the only people who suffer oppression in North Korea or other places. Oppression is typically widespread. Indeed, in Nazi Germany, Christians were oppressed along with Jews, homosexuals, anti-Nazi Germans, and those with handicaps. The Dalits in India are oppressed now,

---

14   David Hawk, "'Thank You Father Kim Il Sung,' Eyewitness Accounts of Severe Violations of Freedom of Thought, Conscience, and Religion in North Korea," U.S. Commission on International Religious Freedom (USCIRF), accessed December 22, 2015, http://www.uscirf .gov/sites/default/files/Thank%20You%20Father%20Kim%20Il%20Sung%20-%20Nov2005.pdf.

and some of them are Christians. Oppression develops after effective forms of persecution have taken root in the psyche of individuals and institutions. If oppression cannot guarantee the eradication of Christians, it attempts instead to at least keep them poor and powerless.

While these definitions will neither end the controversy surrounding persecution nor answer every question raised by the many instances of Christian suffering, they do provide a basic framework for identifying what Christian persecution is. Two kinds of persecution exist: individual and institutional. Many forms of persecution occur. The most prevalent forms are bias, slander, discrimination, incarceration, violence, and oppression. While not exhaustive, this list honors the breadth of persecution forms found throughout the world. The following chapter explores the diversity of the forms of persecution presently taking place around the world.

2

CHRISTIAN PERSECUTION
AROUND THE WORLD TODAY

Behold, I am sending you out as sheep in the midst of
wolves, so be wise as serpents and innocent as doves.
(Matt. 10:16 ESV)

Philosopher Regis Debray, a French revolutionary who went to prison decades ago for fighting alongside Che Guevara in Bolivia, has spent the past ten years of his life decrying the maltreatment of Christians throughout the Middle East. Debray has not converted to Christianity. Politically, he still votes to the left of the left in France, but he remains concerned that Christians — and with them their Christian histories — are being exterminated. Debray is frustrated that Westerners are not paying attention to what is happening to Christians around the world. "Anti-Christian persecution," he writes, "falls squarely into the political blind spot of the West."[1] The aim of this chapter is to help Christians adjust the mirrors of our faith so we can eliminate whatever blind spots we have inherited from our culture.

According to a study recently released by the Pew Research Center, about three-fourths of the population of the world lives under a government that has highly restricted religious freedoms.[2] Of those restrictions, the majority

---

1 John L. Allen, *The Global War on Christians: Dispatches from the Front Lines of Anti-Christian Persecution* (New York: Image, 2013), 16.

2 Pew Forum, "Religious Hostilities Reach a Six-Year High," Pew Research Center

are aimed at Christians.[3] Some international humanitarian agencies have estimated that 80 percent of all religious persecution in the world today is aimed at Christians. The Catholic Bishops Conference estimates that number to be only slightly lower, around 75 percent. Whatever the actual percentage, the reality is undeniable: "Christians are the single most widely persecuted religious group in the world today. This is confirmed in studies by sources as diverse as the Vatican, Open Doors, the Pew Research Center, *Commentary*, *Newsweek*, and the *Economist*."[4] The problem of Christian persecution is vast, involving more than 135 countries.

Before exploring the problem further, I need to make a few observations about the nature of this chapter specifically and about persecution research more generally. While this chapter is not technical, it contains numerous footnotes. The reason is to help readers learn what sources are reliable. Stories of persecution abound. Speculation concerning political agendas and conspiracy theories also abounds. So it seems fair to let the reader know the origins of the stories found here. Hopefully, the chapter will be a resource for future study as well as a source of immediate content related to the persecuted church around the world.

Accurate research on persecution is not easy to obtain for several reasons. First, those committing persecution are, obviously, not interested in reporting it; and those who suffer oftentimes have neither the means nor the time to report what has happened to them. Consider, for instance, this testimony from North Korea (interviewee 37): "A person caught carrying the Bible is doomed. When a person is caught [worshiping], he will be sent to *kwanliso* [prison camp] . . . and the whole family may disappear."[5] Disappearing people are notoriously difficult to count. Thus the nature of the problem mitigates against accurate reporting.

The second reason accurate research on persecution is not easy to obtain is because of a confusion of categories. What counts as persecution, and

---

2014 Annual Report, accessed December 31, 2015, http://www.pewforum.org/files/2014/01/RestrictionsV-full-report.pdf.

3   Allen, *The Global War*; estimate from Martin Lessenthin, chairman of the International Society for Human Rights, 33.

4   Paul Marshall, Lela Gilbert, and Nina Shea, *Persecuted: The Global Assault on Christians* (Nashville: Thomas Nelson, 2013), 4.

5   Michael Cromartie, chair, USCIRF, "Prison Without Bars: Refugee and Defector Testimonies of Severe Violations of Freedom of Religion or Belief in North Korea" (2008), 40.

what is political oppression? When the Muslim Sudanese government in the north attacks and razes Christian and animist villages in the south, is the government guilty of persecuting Christians? True, hundreds of thousands of Christians were slaughtered in the Sudanese Civil War. However, thousands of animists and other non-Christians were killed at the same time. Their villages were targeted, too. In what category do the dead Christians of Sudan fit — victims of political oppression or victims of persecution?

There are many other such questions related to categories of suffering. What is legitimate criminal punishment, and what is an abuse of the law for the purpose of persecuting an evangelist? Stories abound that describe successful evangelists being arrested and charged with gun smuggling, spying, or stealing — often evidence is planted in their homes or in their vehicles to substantiate the charges. Even more to the point, what happens when Christians actually defy the law and proselytize their neighbors or smuggle Bibles into forbidden places? When is the arrest an act of justice, and when is it institutional persecution?

The apostle Peter warns against suffering as a criminal or an evildoer. He makes plain that Christ's blessing is for those who suffer on account of Christ — not those who suffer for being criminals (1 Peter 3:13–17). Where exactly is that line drawn? One may be imprisoned, tortured, or killed for a principle or a cause, but that suffering may not necessarily be the suffering of a martyr. There are countless examples of people suffering and dying on principle (think about the Civil Rights movement or the actions of Dietrich Bonhoeffer). Such suffering may or may not have been the result of Christian persecution. Clear-cut categories are definitely needed in order to guarantee accurate figures concerning the scope of the Christian persecution problem. And, biblically speaking, such categories are needed so suffering saints can with confidence receive the blessings Christ promises for the persecuted.

Not only are persecution statistics affected by the lack of reporting and by the confusion of categories, but also because of a third reason: apathy. Few outlets pay attention to Christian persecution. One need not be overly critical to notice the barrenness of reporting by secular media on behalf of Christians. One can fairly say that there is "a reflexive hostility to institutional religion, especially Christianity, in some sectors of secular opinion. People conditioned by such views are inclined to see Christianity as the agent of repression, not its victim."[6] Secular media, it seems, have a hard time tracking what they don't believe exists.

While John Allen notes the easily explained absence of reporting on Christian persecution by secular outlets, he has a harder time explaining the absence of reporting by Christian sources. He offers four reasons Christians are not tracking the suffering of brothers and sisters around the world. First, Christians in America and in the West simply don't identify with the persecuted church. How can an American Christian relate to someone like Christianah Oluwatoyin Oluwasesin, who was beaten and burned to death because she was a Christian teacher in a Muslim school in Nigeria? We have an extremely difficult time relating to what seems so fantastic and so unreal; thus we aren't sure what to do with the information once we receive it. More important, we don't go looking for it in the first place.

The second reason Christians are silent about investigating, reporting, and researching Christian persecution is that the topic itself is disconcerting. By nature, persecution challenges shallow faith and comfortable Christianity. From my own experience of raising awareness for the persecuted church over the past fifteen years, I can affirm that many Christians — including pastors — are not comfortable hearing about persecution. While from a doctrinal perspective, we decry health-and-wealth, prosperity preaching, we naturally prefer a Christian experience that is comfortable and safe for the whole family. Why focus on an issue if it makes us so uncomfortable? It's easier to leave the matter alone.

Third, Christian persecution is a neglected topic of study and research because it requires hard work and serious resources to discover. Christian entities in the West tend to use their resources in other ways and cannot fathom expending exorbitant amounts of cash to study persecution on the islands of Indonesia or in the sub-Saharan countries of Africa. Because Christian resources are limited, it becomes difficult to amass a network of correspondents able to report persecution in every corner of the earth.

Fourth, Christians also suffer the malady of "good cause" fatigue. Because no one is talking much about persecution, it gets displaced by other, more celebrated Christian causes: evangelism, missions, unreached people groups, church planting, church growth, poverty, pro-life issues, and other political

---

6   Allen, *The Global War*, 15.

concerns. In short, persecution isn't really on the American Christian radar as a church priority.

So, as Allen notes, for these four reasons — and probably for others that have not been mentioned — Christian persecution research is lacking. Nevertheless, the news is not all bad. A growing number of Christian and secular groups are starting to pay closer attention to the suffering of Christ's body.

A few organizations stand out. Three of the more popular ministries with long records of dedicated service to the persecuted church are Voice of the Martyrs (www.persecution.com), Open Doors (www.opendoors.org), and the Barnabas Fund (www.barnabasfund.org), the latter of which operates out of the United Kingdom.

There are also research agencies dedicated (at least partially) to discovering the extent to which Christians are being persecuted around the world. The largest and most respected of these is the Pew Research Center, particularly the center's Religion and Public Life Project, which publishes an annual report each January detailing religious hostilities around the world (www .pewforum.org).

In addition to the Pew Research Center's work, the following entities also document Christian persecution on a global scale:

- USCIRF (www.uscirf.gov) is a bipartisan commission that produces an annual report to the Congress of the United States detailing issues from around the world germane to religious freedom.
- Morningstar News (www.morningstar.org) is an independent news agency dedicated solely to reporting news on Christian persecution. I feature their newsfeed at my blog (www.GregoryCCochran.com).
- WorldWatch Monitor (www.worldwatchmonitor.org) is another news agency that focuses on the worldwide persecution of Christians.
- Forum 18 (www.forum18.org) is a Norwegian human-rights organization that covers religious freedom all over the world, but focuses primarily on the former Soviet countries. The name is derived from Article 18 of the UN Declaration of Human Rights, which promises freedom of religion.
- The Hudson Institute Center for Religious Freedom (http://crf .hudson.org) provides publications, op-eds, and information related to religious freedom in the United States and around the world.

- China Aid (www.chinaaid.org) is a human-rights organization focused on religious liberty issues in China. Founder Bob Fu was instrumental in negotiating the escape and eventual release of the blind legal activist Chen Guangcheng in 2012.
- The Center for the Global Study of Christianity is a research institution that works diligently to uncover accurate demographic data "to the ends of the earth." This center is an outgrowth of work begun by David Barrett and his *World Christian Encyclopedia* research. This center resides on the campus of Gordon-Conwell Theological Seminary (http://www.gordonconwell.edu/resources/Center-for-the-Study-of-Global-Christianity.cfm).
- The Southern Baptist Convention's Ethics and Religious Liberty Commission (www.erlc.com) provides information about and raises awareness of religious liberty issues in the United States and around the world.

In addition to the ministries and research entities mentioned above, two recent books provide helpful information regarding the global crisis of Christian persecution. The first is John Allen's *The Global War on Christians: Dispatches from the Front Lines of Anti-Christian Persecution*. Allen, the senior Vatican analyst for CNN, writes from personal experience, detailing individual accounts of suffering he has seen firsthand as a reporter in situations of intense persecution.

The other book is *Persecuted: The Global Assault on Christians*, written by Paul Marshall, Lela Gilbert, and Nina Shea, each of whom has affiliation with the Hudson Institute.[7] In addition to producing a riveting book detailing the global persecution of Christians, these three authors — under the auspices of the Hudson Institute's Center for Religious Freedom — operate the website Persecution Report (www.persecutionreport.org) to keep Christians up to date concerning persecution throughout the various regions of the world. Much of the following information has been adapted from these two books.

So what persecution is happening around the world to Christians? In short, Christians are suffering in numbers exceeding historic proportions. For reasons outlined above, the numbers are often difficult to discover. So the

---

7   See note 4, above.

estimates of annual martyrdom vary widely from a low of 7,300 per year to a high exceeding 100,000 annually. Allen asserts that half of all martyrdoms in Christian history occurred in the twentieth century: "Fully half, or forty-five million, went to their deaths in the twentieth century, most of them falling victim to either Communism or National Socialism. More Christians were killed because of their faith in the twentieth century than in all previous centuries combined."[8]

Again, the numbers are not as precise as one might hope, but there is no doubt that Christians are suffering torture, imprisonment, and death in unparalleled numbers:

> Christians today are, by some order of magnitude, the most persecuted religious body on the planet, suffering not just martyrdom but all the forms of intimidation and oppression . . . in record numbers. That's not a hunch, or a theory, or an anecdotal impression, but an undisputed empirical fact of life. Confirmation comes from multiple sources, all respected observers of either the human rights scene or the global religious landscape.[9]

In several so-called hotspots, Christians are literally in danger of becoming extinct. In *Persecuted*, the authors write: "Over the past one hundred years, according to a range of estimates, the Christian presence has declined in Iraq from 35 percent to 1.5 percent; in Iran from 15 percent to 2 percent; in Syria from 40 percent to 10 percent; in Turkey from 32 percent to 0.15 percent. Among the most significant factors explaining this decline is religious persecution."[10] And the massive destruction done by ISIS in Iraq and Syria has Eliza Griswold asking in *The New York Times Magazine*, "Is This the End of Christianity in the Middle East?"[11] Griswold laments that ISIS and other extremist groups are enslaving, killing, and uprooting Christians with no apparent end in sight.

However bad the scenarios above may be, the situation in Nigeria is

---

8   Allen, *The Global War*, 33.
9   Allen, *The Global War*, 33.
10   Marshall, Gilbert, and Shea, *Persecuted*, 6.
11   Eliza Griswold, "Is This the End of Christianity in the Middle East?" *The New York Times Magazine*, July 22, 2015.

worse. Nigeria — especially northern Nigeria — has been a dangerous place to be a Christian. At a panel discussion sponsored by the Hudson Institute in November 2013, Ann Buwalda, executive director for the Jubilee Campaign (www.jubileecampaign.org), declared that, according to the organization's research, Nigeria produced 60 percent of all martyrs in 2012 — more than the number of martyrs in Pakistan, Syria, Kenya, and Egypt combined.

In Nigeria, the problem is particularly acute, as Muslims in the north have been fighting with Christians in the south for decades. The problem has intensified of late because of "the increased influence of radical Islam, manifested especially in two trends. One has been the overt attempt to apply Islamic law nationwide; the other, which is overlapping, is the growth of Islamic militias."[12]

One Islamic militia in particular has been devastatingly deadly in Nigeria: Boko Haram, a group recently named an official terrorist organization by the U.S. Department of State. In October 2012, an armed militia — believed by experts to be Boko Haram — attacked the Federal Polytechnic College in the town of Mubi, in the state of Adamawa, Nigeria. Actually, three different schools were attacked that weekend, with a death toll estimated (by AllAfrica) to exceed forty-six students.

At the Federal Polytechnic College alone, more than two dozen students were killed. Particularly harrowing in this incident is how the murders took place. The attack was by night, when students were either studying or sleeping. Students were brought out of their apartments and separated. The Christians — who were called out by name — were then executed, either by having their throats slit or being shot in the head. According to a spokesman from Open Doors, this area of Nigeria has suffered violence every day since 2011. With such ongoing violence, Nigeria may be, as the Hudson Institute has said, the most dangerous place on earth to be a Christian.

Unfortunately, Nigeria is but one of several places in stiff competition for such a dishonorable designation. Consider the small, desert country of Eritrea, located in the Horn of Africa along the Red Sea. One of the worst human rights atrocities of our day is taking place in the Me'eter Prison, with the full knowledge of the watching world. Me'eter Prison was opened

---

12   Marshall, Gilbert, and Shea, *Persecuted*, 239.

in 2009, basically to serve as "a concentration camp for Christians."[13] The atrocities described there have been documented by WikiLeaks since 2011. Inmates are forced to live in cargo containers so crowded they are never able to lie down. They have no protection from the searing heat during the day (often exceeding 110 degrees Fahrenheit) and no recourse from the cold at night. Arid desert climates can experience 50 degree temperature changes from day to night. Inmates may die from starvation, dehydration, heatstroke, cholera, diphtheria, or other infectious diseases.

The inmates who survive the deplorable conditions are subjected to other forms of torture and abuse. Stories abound of sexual abuse and physical beatings. Even the work and exercise prescribed are forms of torture — such as counting the grains of sand in a certain area during the noonday heat or squatting to move rocks from one side of one's body to the other, repeated endlessly.

Again, affirming Regis Debray's distressing point, such abuse falls into the blind spot of Western academics and media elites. The atrocities at Me'eter are documented in books, on WikiLeaks, via Internet sources, and through activists like gospel singer Helen Berhane, herself an inmate at a prison in Eritrea from 2004 to 2006 because of her faith in Christ.

The information is available for those adequately concerned, but who is worried about persecuted Christians? Certainly not the U.K. Border Agency. Berhane was scheduled to speak to a Release International gathering in the United Kingdom on behalf of other persecuted Christians, but she was denied entry by the U.K. Border Agency. Parliament passed unanimously Early Day Motion 1531 in support of Berhane (and condemning the Border Agency decision), but she was not allowed entry to tell her story in person. And Christians still languish in putrid prison conditions in Eritrea on account of Christ.

Another nation vying for worst place on earth to be a Christian is North Korea. According to *Persecuted*, "North Korea is the most militantly atheistic country in the world."[14] For the past fifty years, North Korea has sought (somewhat successfully) to eradicate Christianity from the country. "Nearly

---

13   Quote and following Me'eter description from Allen, *The Global War*, 1–4.

14   Marshall, Gilbert, and Shea, *Persecuted*, 52. The description of North Korea is taken largely from this book (pp. 52–62), with supplementation from other sources.

all outward vestiges of religion have been wiped out, and what exists is under tight government control."[15]

USCIRF has produced the most extensive research to date on the status of Christians and Christianity in North Korea. One report is titled "A Prison Without Bars," obviously alluding to the fact that the entire country is a giant prison cell for its inhabitants. A humanitarian aid industry has cropped up along the border lands of China and North Korea, hoping to help North Korean refugees escape their oppression and find Jesus Christ. As a result, the North Korean government has been training officials to pose as Christians and as pastors in order to infiltrate these Christian and humanitarian groups and uncover the identities of North Korean Christians.

The report of this situation is sober in assessing the severity of the maltreatment incurred by Christians. Indicative of the overall animus against Christianity is the story told by interviewee 20 in the USCIRF report:

> There was even a case of a child (16 years old). That kid was the same age as my kid. They made that kid stand on the platform, in front of gathered parents. They declared that it is a big problem how teenagers cross the river too often and how they spread rumors about God. There, the kid's entire family was arrested in order to show an example. It happened in 2003 at Yuseon boys' middle school. According to the rumor, that kid had learnt whole Bible scriptures by heart and that was the reason he was arrested. He stayed in China for eight months and got caught. And because of religion, he and his family were all arrested.[16]

Such stories abound — some more heinous. According to one soldier interviewed by a human rights organization about the persecution he witnessed, his unit "rounded up the church's pastor, two assistant pastors, and two elders. The five bound men were placed in front of the bulldozer and given a final opportunity to renounce their Christian faith. When they refused, they were crushed to death in front of other members of the church."[17] Not all stories from North Korea are so gruesome, of course, but the situation

---

15   Marshall, Gilbert, and Shea, *Persecuted*, 52.
16   Cromartie, "Prison Without Bars," 27.
17   Allen, *The Global War*, 84.

there is bad enough that the country has been at the top of Open Doors' World Watch List for eleven years in a row.

As terrible as the situation has become in North Korea, the result is not defeat for Christ or his kingdom. Sketchy reports pieced together indicate that even in North Korea, the church of Jesus Christ is growing. "There is emerging evidence that, at great risk, there are small Christian gatherings in private homes that may collectively encompass hundreds of thousands of people."[18] But one USCIRF interviewee (34) thinks an underground church would be impossible in North Korea:

> Underground *believers* would be a more appropriate term than underground *church*. Church would be something like a place where people can gather and listen to a sermon, but it's impossible to exist for long. Instead, underground believers can exist. There is a chance that two people pair up and hold their hands together to pray. However, a gathering of three or more is dangerous.[19]

Though egregious violations of basic human rights abound in North Korea, Nigeria, and Eritrea, these countries are not alone in their severe maltreatment of the bride of Christ. The Middle East, too, abounds with horrendous mistreatment of Christians on account of Christ.

Statistics were quoted earlier to demonstrate the demise of Christianity throughout the Middle East. Perhaps the only aspect of Christian suffering throughout the Middle East that is more stunning than its magnitude is the enormous silence on the part of world leaders. This is not to say that no one is speaking out. Many are sounding the alarm, as we have seen. But the scope of suffering is startling. Ayaan Hirsi Ali, not exactly a Christian apologist, said in a 2012 *Newsweek* article, "From one end of the Muslim world to the other, Christians are being murdered for their faith."[20] Hirsi Ali, like John Allen and others who study Muslim violence against Christians in the Middle East, has offered possible explanations for the relative silence of

---

18   Marshall, Gilbert, and Shea, *Persecuted*, 59.

19   Cromartie, "Prison Without Bars," 21. Also quoted in Marshall, Gilbert, and Shea, *Persecuted*, 59.

20   Ayaan Hirsi Ali, "The Global War on Christians in the Muslim World," *Newsweek*, February 6, 2012.

Westerners on behalf of Christians. One of her primary explanations for the lack of support Christians receive from the media is the fear that reporting negatively on Islamic violence might beget further violence. Yet Hirsi Ali forcefully concludes, "The conspiracy of silence surrounding this violent expression of religious intolerance has to stop. Nothing less than the fate of Christianity — and ultimately of all religious minorities — in the Islamic world is at stake."[21]

Silence is certainly a problem, but so, too, is the confusion of categories. Islamic violence in the Middle East is not targeted solely against Christians. In Bahrain, for example, the large increase in religious hostility (noted by the Pew Research Center) had more to do with Sunni Muslims discriminating against Shia Muslims. According to the center, "Shia Muslims were vilified in the state-run media, and thousands were dismissed from public- and private-sector jobs. The government also destroyed Shia mosques and other places of worship."[22]

An important point for Christians to remember when discussing the Middle East (and North Africa) is that the matter is more complicated than a simple hatred of Christianity. With that said, however, the demise of Christianity is both drastic and devastating for religious freedom. Christians, as noted in the title of an article in *The Telegraph*, are close to extinction in the Middle East: "Christianity faces being wiped out of the 'biblical heartlands' in the Middle East because of mounting persecution of worshipers."[23]

In the Middle East (and the northern tier of Africa), Arab Christians made up 20 percent of the population at the turn of the twentieth century. "Today, however, that vibrant Arab Christianity feels like a dying species. Christianity now represents just 5 percent of the population, no more than twelve million people, and current projections show that number dropping to six million people by the middle of the century."[24] In Afghanistan, Christians are a negligible portion of the overall population, but they seem to be

---

21 Hirsi Ali, "The Global War."

22 Pew Research Center, "Arab Spring Restrictions on Religion Findings," accessed January 31, 2014, http://www.pewforum.org/2013/06/20/arab-spring-restrictions-on-religion -findings/#harassment-of-specific-groups.

23 Edward Malnick, "Christianity 'Close to Extinction' in Middle East," *The Telegraph*, December 23, 2012.

24 Allen, *The Global War*, 117.

a constant focus of attention for the Taliban and some governing authorities there. Christians can be arrested and killed for converting from Islam. The Taliban has vowed to eliminate the tiny population of Christians (maybe 2,500) and also eradicate any influence Christianity has in the country, including targeting humanitarian agencies with ties to Christianity.

In Egypt, the situation continues spiraling toward a crisis. In February 2011, when the United States called for an orderly transition away from Hosni Mubarak's reign in the country, many hopefuls were calling it an Arab Spring. Now, more than a few editorials have referred to the aftermath as an Arab Winter, or, more accurately, a Christian Winter of Destruction. Religious freedom — particularly freedom of the Christian religion — has suffered great loss in Egypt. By the end of April 2011, USCIRF recommended to Secretary of State Hillary Clinton that Egypt be classified as a Country of Particular Concern (CPC). The main reason was the dramatic increase in violations of religious freedom against Christians.

In Iran, both severe persecution and a measure of hope exist. There are indications of a healthy underground church. In addition, the year 2013 brought an election in which a moderate president, Hassan Rowhani, was elected, promising protection for all minority religions. But the country itself is actually run by Ayatollah Ali Khamenei, who in the past has referred to Christians as the enemies of Islam and has warned the Iranian people of the threat of Christianity's spread in the country. The government severely restricts Christian freedom, does not allow the Bible to be printed in Farsi, limits college to those who declare Islamic orthodoxy, and does not protect Muslims who convert to Christianity. Converts can be killed with no legal ramifications.

In Iraq, the situation is bleak. Since the ouster of Saddam Hussein in 2003, Iraq has seen two-thirds of its Christian population flee to other countries. Legend has it that the apostle Thomas founded a church in what is now Iraq, indicating the long history of gospel faith in that region of the world. Yet, "the one-two punch of Sunni and Shia extremism, combined with deep governmental discrimination and indifference, now threatens the very existence of Iraq's ancient Christian churches. Some of these still pray in Aramaic, the language of Jesus of Nazareth."[25] The situation in Iraq was bad

---

25   Marshall, Gilbert, and Shea, *Persecuted*, 229.

after 2003, but it grew much worse in October 2010. On that day, Our Lady of Perpetual Help Church — a Syrian Catholic church in Baghdad — was attacked during a worship service. Nearly sixty parishioners and priests were killed and scores of others were injured, including children as young as age 3. By the end of that year, Joseph Kassab, the executive director of the Chaldean Federation of America, wrote, "Things are deteriorating very fast in Iraq; our people are left with no choice but to flee because they are losing hope and there is no serious action taken to protect them as of today."[26] Even the honorable and courageous Andrew White, called the Vicar of Baghdad, has had to leave the country by order of the Archbishop of Canterbury because of imminent danger.

Iraq is not the only Middle Eastern country in which Christians are losing hope. Allen writes, "Today there's tremendous fear among Christian leaders that Syria will be the next Iraq, meaning the next Middle Eastern nation where a police state falls and Christians become the primary victims of the ensuing chaos."[27] Hundreds of thousands — if not more than a million — Christians have fled their homes and villages in Syria. One of the hardest hit areas is Homs, where 90 percent of the Christian population have been killed or expelled. Homes and property have been confiscated, and, according to many reports, the Christians become targets if they head to one of the refugee centers set up by the UN. So these Christians are, literally, homeless and desperate. Safe spaces are a rare luxury for them anywhere in the Middle East. Attacks against Christians have become fairly common over the past eight years.

In Saudi Arabia, the situation is less violent, but even more oppressive. Saudi Arabia is a total Muslim state. No other churches are allowed. No open manifestations of Christianity are tolerated. Even private prayer meetings are shut down and participants punished by beatings or possibly even killed. According to Saudi law, all citizens must be Muslim. "In March 2012, Saudi Arabia's Grand Mufti Abdulaziz ibn Abdullah Al al-Sheikh . . . issued a religious fatwa declaring it 'necessary to destroy all the churches' in the region, including those outside of Saudi Arabia itself."[28] Suffice it to say, the

---

26 Marshall, Gilbert, and Shea, *Persecuted*, 237.
27 Allen, *The Global War*, 142.
28 As quoted in Marshall, Gilbert, and Shea, *Persecuted*, 156.

kingdom of Saudi Arabia seeks to squelch any reference to the kingdom of our Lord Jesus Christ.

Stopping the conversation here seems something like stopping a trans-American road trip in Salinas, Kansas — there is so much more left to see. There are yet other parts of the Muslim world where violence against Christians is intense: Pakistan, Indonesia, Morocco, and Somalia. And there has been no sustained discussion of the continued efforts of Communist governments in Vietnam, Laos, and Cuba to eradicate faith. By sheer numbers, more persecution is happening in China than in any nation on earth. There are more Christians in prison in China than in any other place.

In South Asia, Christians are persecuted heavily in Bhutan, Nepal, and Sri Lanka. In 2008, Orissa State in India became a violent hotspot in which Christians of all denominations living in the area had to run for their lives:

[Hindu] mobs killed at least forty people and burned thousands of houses, hundreds of churches, and thirteen educational institutions. During the attacks, a large number of women and girls were victims of sexual violence. Nearly two years later, about sixty of the area's women were found in Delhi. They had been sold into sexual slavery. The attacks led to ten thousand fleeing from their homes.[29]

There is violence against Christians all over the world. This brief overview is intended to portray only the magnitude of the problem. Obviously, this chapter focuses only on the persecution of Christians. Muslims are persecuted, too. In fact, Islam is the second-most persecuted religious group in the world — often the persecution is carried out by other Muslim groups in the name of "true Islam." But Muslims suffer. And by proportion of population, ethnic Jews are persecuted perhaps more than any other group. The world has an awful problem establishing religious freedom. But for Christians, there are unique considerations. Nearly every New Testament writer speaks of persecution, Jude being the lone example to the contrary. Because it is tied to the presence of Christ, persecution is endemic to the gospel.

Whatever the reason has been for Christians to neglect this important subject, let's take from this chapter a hunger and an appetite to eliminate

---

29 Marshall, Gilbert, and Shea, *Persecuted*, 91.

our own blind spots and take up the biblical command to remember our brothers and sisters suffering for Christ. We are connected in Christ to those who suffer for righteousness. To understand better why persecution is so prevalent around the world, we must turn our attention to the Bible — and specifically to the instructions given to us by Christ himself.

However, before exploring the New Testament instruction on persecution, we should journey a bit through the Old Testament. The logic of this approach is simple: before a farmer harvests his crops, he must first work the soil. In the same way, we must now till up the ground of the Old Testament in order to harvest what has grown to full flower with the coming of Christ in the New Testament.

PART 2

THE BIBLICAL PORTRAIT OF PERSECUTION

3

THE GENESIS OF PERSECUTION AND MARTYRDOM:

STEPHEN OR ABEL?

Sin is crouching at the door. Its desire is for you, but you must rule over it.

(Gen. 4:7 ESV)

Where in the Scriptures does the conversation on persecution begin? Perhaps it begins with the first martyr mentioned in the Bible. But who is the first martyr?

When I speak on behalf of the persecuted church, I often ask, "Who is the first martyr in the Bible?" I always get the answer, "Stephen!" That response makes sense; it comes from our Sunday school lessons and catechism questions. My own children grew up under the tutelage of the *1777 New England Primer,* which was the first textbook used in American schools. The *Primer,* a catechism of biblical theology as much as a book of grammar and elementary instruction, asks the question, "Who is the first martyr?" The answer: "Stephen is the first Christian martyr."

While technically correct, that answer sounds incomplete. Stephen is the first martyr *after* Christ (see Acts 7), but he is not the first martyr. Christ himself is the first *Christian* martyr, right? After all, if one wishes to understand martyrdom and how to respond to persecution, he would logically go back to Christ's example, not Stephen's. The apostle Paul makes this point in his encouragement to young Timothy to remain steadfast in the faith. The apostle reminds Timothy that it was Christ who testified the good confession before Pontius Pilate (1 Tim. 6:13). Paul is saying, therefore, that it was Christ who first proved to be a faithful witness (martyr) in the face of the turbulence of persecution.

When, like Paul, we speak of a witness as a person who holds to his testimony in spite of persecution, then we are speaking of a *martyr*. The word "martyr" is an English word derived from the original Greek word, *martus*, meaning simply "a witness." In the early church, just as today, "witness" means someone who has pertinent information and, so, might be called on to testify according to that knowledge. "Witnessing," for Christians, is simply offering testimony about our knowledge of God. For Christians, then, Christ is the *proto-martyr*, the first and best exemplar of a Christian response to persecution. We venerate Christ, not Stephen.

Think of it this way. If you wanted to learn to play quarterback for a football team, whom would you consult, Peyton Manning or one of your friends who had been coached by Manning? Even if your friend were knowledgeable and skilled, you would still prefer to go directly to the perennial all-pro quarterback himself, rather than learning secondhand from someone else, right? The same is true (but even more so!) when it comes to learning about persecution. As Christians, we go directly to the main source: Christ. Stephen was a faithful martyr, but he obviously followed Christ's example (and exemplified Christ's spirit).

So, it's logical that we should start our biblical discussion of persecution with the martyrdom of Christ. Yet, starting with Christ leaves a great deal unsaid about other people of God who suffered for their faith before Christ. What about John the Baptist? He was a faithful witness before Herod, and it cost him his head. Even before John the Baptist, Christ, and Stephen, there were martyrs in the Old Testament. Legend has it that the prophet Isaiah was put inside a log and sawn in two (perhaps explaining the comment in Heb. 11:37). There were many faithful witnesses in the Old Testament who were persecuted to death (see Matt. 23:35). How do they fit in a full-orbed biblical understanding of Christian persecution?

In Matthew 23:34–35, Jesus makes plain that he is intimately connected to all those martyrs from the Old Testament who spilled their blood by faith.

> Therefore, behold, I am sending you prophets and wise men and scribes; some of them you will kill and crucify, and some of them you will scourge

in your synagogues, and persecute from city to city, so that upon you may fall the guilt of all the righteous blood shed on earth, from the blood of righteous Abel to the blood of Zechariah, the son of Berechiah, whom you murdered between the temple and the altar.

Jesus refers to all the saints who suffered persecution in the past as suffering on account of righteousness. He lumps together the faithful who suffered under the category of "righteous blood." Jesus also connects the Old Testament saints of the past with all those who would be persecuted in the future on account of being his people:

Blessed are those who have been persecuted for the sake of righteousness, for theirs is the kingdom of heaven. Blessed are you when people insult you and persecute you, and falsely say all kinds of evil against you because of Me. Rejoice and be glad, for your reward in heaven is great; for in the same way they persecuted the prophets who were before you. (Matt. 5:10–12)

A connection clearly exists between the prophets of old who were persecuted and later Christians who suffer on account of Christ. This is because "following Jesus is the path of righteousness."[1] Thus, discussions of persecution and martyrdom must focus on Christ and the path of righteousness. Somehow, the conversation ought also to include the saints of the Old Testament.

With the understanding that Christ is central to all persecution — past, present, and future — we can return to our original question and ask where in the Bible the first instance of persecution is. Who is the first martyr in biblical history that is on the path of righteousness?

As it turns out, persecution is first found in the book of Genesis. In fact, martyrdom begins with the first murder in the Bible — the murder of Abel by his brother Cain. Abel, therefore, is the first faithful witness persecuted to death for the sake of righteousness.

The Cain and Abel saga is recorded in Genesis 4. There it states that both Cain and Abel made offerings to the Lord, with Abel's offering as pleasing

---

1   Grant Osborne, *Matthew*, Zondervan Exegetical Commentary on the New Testament (Grand Rapids: Zondervan, 2010), 170.

to the Lord as Anna Grace's offering was a delight to her father. Cain's offering, on the other hand, was not accepted by God. Think about that. Cain gathered a portion of his crops and brought them to the place of offering; he gave up his crops as an offering of worship to the Lord, only to find out that the offering was not accepted.

Genesis 4 does not tell us specifically why God rejected Cain's offering. Some have speculated that the rejection was based on Cain's offering crops instead of livestock (as Abel offered). But that is just conjecture. While it is true that Abel offered livestock and that God accepted Abel's offering, it is also true that those two statements taken together do not necessarily mean that God's rejection of Cain's offering was based primarily on the elements.

To illustrate the fallacy of judging by such outward appearance, I think of two boys I once knew. The younger boy was passionate and high-spirited. He could have been a cheerleader, but he much preferred to couple his emotions with actions like wrestling, fighting, and playing sports. His older brother (who was probably 5 or 6 at the time of this incident) had a way of using his little brother's energy to his advantage. If the older brother wanted something, he would get his younger brother all worked up to go ask for it from Mom and Dad.

On one occasion, the older brother wanted to spend the night with me and my wife. So he got his younger brother to ask if it might be possible. The older brother was shocked when the answer was no. The next thing we saw was the younger of the two running through the hallway toward the adults at the table, bawling and dejected. The little guy left a stream of tears down the hallway, which likely would have pooled beneath his feet when he arrived at the table, but he didn't stay at the table with the adults long enough. The instant he arrived, he smacked his mother across the back and screamed, "Mean mommy!"

What happened next shocked me and my wife. Both parents, without hesitation, marched past the aggressive little screamer and went to the older brother, who was promptly disciplined. For some time, the scene confused us until we got the whole story. Parents know their children, and these parents knew that the older brother had instigated the entire affair. It's not as though the younger boy was innocent, but the older brother was primarily to blame for misleading his little brother and stoking him to commit a crime of sorts against his parents.

The point of the story is simply this. Just as parents know better than to judge based only on outward actions, so too God knows to judge beyond mere appearances. Even more, God knows how to judge, with precision, the thoughts and intentions of our hearts (see Eccl. 12:14; Heb. 4:12). As parents, we often fail. By outward appearances, the little boy was guilty and the elder boy innocent. In reality, however, they both were guilty — and the elder more so because he wrongly manipulated his unsuspecting little brother.

Cain and Abel presented two different offerings. Would God have been obligated to accept Cain's offering if it were exactly the same as Abel's? No. There is a time later in the Old Testament in which Saul offered an animal sacrifice to the Lord (just as Abel had offered in Gen. 4). In response, the Lord rebuked Saul and sent word through Samuel that the kingdom would no longer belong to Saul, but to another king (David) whom God would choose (1 Sam. 13:5–14). Saul's sacrifice of an animal was sin against God. In this instance, Saul — like Abel — offered an animal sacrifice, but the Lord was displeased with it. So the Old Testament looks beyond the mere substance of the sacrifice itself to find which offerings are pleasing to the Lord. The issue is not what is sacrificed. Rather, the issue is who is making the offering, and why the offering is made.

So the difference between Cain and Abel is not found in the item, but in their disposition. Why are they offering anything to God? One seems to be making an offering based on self-righteousness, while the other is making his offering by faith in worship to God on account of God's righteousness. In other words, one of these brothers is righteous, while the other is not. In his commentary on the Genesis 4 account, Kenneth Matthews explains Cain this way:

> In the New Testament, Cain is viewed as the forefather of an unrighteous seed who had drawn first blood in the perpetual struggle between the ungodly and the godly seed first anticipated in 3:15. According to the custom of primogeniture, the firstborn received the bounty of parental inheritance (Deut. 21:17), but from the viewpoint of Genesis as a whole, it is not surprising that the firstborn in whom Adam and Eve had so much hope would be refused for another. This rejection of the firstborn for the younger son (in this case Seth) portends the common pattern witnessed among the patriarchs where the custom of primogeniture is superseded

by divine election and the outworking of covenant promise. God's gracious dealings with Israel also were initiated by his elective love (Deut.
4:37; 7:7–8), but the Mosaic covenant included moral demands. Israel's
acceptance was not automatic due to their status as God's firstborn. Cain
and his unrighteous offspring served as a reminder to Israel that its des-
tiny was measured in the scales of ethical behavior.[2]

Matthews demonstrates that Cain must have thought he was entitled to
God's acceptance on account of his being the firstborn son. Thus, he was
enraged at hearing of God's disapproval. Abel, then, represents the first in
a series of surprising reversals of fortune in which the righteous emerge by
God's choice rather than by the normal firstborn status: Isaac is chosen over
Ishmael; Jacob over Esau; Joseph over his brothers; Ephraim over Manasseh;
David over his seven brothers — and over Saul. In David, of course, the Old
Testament reaches its zenith. God's people have the Promised Land under
the authority of their God-appointed king who, like Abel, is a shepherd.

Whether Cain thought he merited God's favor on account of being the
firstborn or whether his arrogance came about for some other reason, the
truth is plain that he counted himself righteous.[3] Genesis 4:5 says, "So Cain
became very angry and his countenance fell." The presence of anger here is
a clear indication of self-righteousness. Cain's response is an early personi-
fication of the warning later written in James 1:20: "The anger of man does
not achieve the righteousness of God." Instead, anger demonstrates self-
righteousness, as with Cain who furiously sensed that God acted improperly.
Imagine that — Cain felt as though he were being treated unfairly by God!
Such a notion is ludicrous — that God would not judge rightly. Who knows
best what is acceptable worship, Cain or God?

Furthermore, if you remember the story of Anna Grace seeking to please
her father, then you will also understand that Cain's desire must not have

---

2   Kenneth A. Matthews, *Genesis 1–11:26*, The New American Commentary (Nashville:
Broadman and Holman, 1996), 269.

3   See Gordon J. Wenham, *Genesis 1–15*, Word Biblical Commentary (Waco, TX: Word,
1987), 104, for a review of the five common interpretations of the motive driving Cain to murder his brother. I am asserting that the narrative be interpreted from the fuller, New Testament
viewpoint of justification by faith. The righteous people of faith suffer persecution at the hands
of the unrighteous (cf. Matt. 23:34–36; John 15:19; Heb. 11:4; 1 John 3:11–13).

been to "please" God, but to get God off his back by doing what God demanded. Why do I say this? What do you think would have happened if Anna Grace's father would have rejected her song and said, "I am not happy with this"? Anna Grace's sparkling blue eyes would have appeared less like Christmas lights and more like swimming pools, as the tears surely would have flowed into them, spilling over her eyelashes, and down her red and flushed cheeks. Anna Grace would not have gotten angry at her father. She would have been broken and sad. She would have sought to bridge the gap and find out how to make things right again with her dad. Nothing remotely familiar to such contrition is attributed to Cain. Instead, Cain seeks to justify himself before God. His ire burns against God.

Judging from his violent actions, Cain obviously felt justified in this wrath against God, but how is one ever justified in the sight of God? Cain and Abel lived after the Fall with its curse of sin and death. Thus, neither Cain nor Abel could ever have been righteous before God. If they were ever to be acceptable in the sight of God, they would need to depend on God's gracious provision for them. God would have to cover them somehow, the way he had covered Adam and Eve after they fell into sin and brought the curse of death into the world. God killed an animal and with its skin covered the nakedness of Adam and Eve (Gen. 3:21). Likewise, Cain and Abel both stood in desperate need of God's covering for them. Their only hope was grace. And their only claim to grace was their faith, believing that somehow God would mercifully supply a life-covering for their otherwise dead souls. Offerings to the Lord, therefore, were faith offerings. Faith offerings cannot obligate God, and they are an expression of love to God, believing in hope that God has provided everything sinners need to have a relationship with him.

Cain's offering did not hint of such faith. Instead, Cain represents self-righteousness against the righteousness of God. Thus, God confronts Cain and warns him: "Then the LORD said to Cain, 'Why are you angry? And why has your countenance fallen? If you do well, will not your countenance be lifted up? And if you do not do well, sin is crouching at the door; and its desire is for you, but you must master it'" (Gen. 4:6–7). Cain did not master sin but instead persisted in his self-righteousness. Instead of repenting before the Lord, seeking forgiveness and reconciliation, Cain went to Abel in the field, told him about God's warning, and then killed him. His murder proved both that sin had conquered him (instead of the reverse) and that he felt justified in holding God in contempt, carrying out an execution against his own brother. In self-righteousness, Cain spurned the counsel of God and targeted his own brother for murder, ultimately because God had counted his younger brother as righteous. Cain acted as though silencing Abel (created in the image of God) would somehow simultaneously silence God too. Abel was the immediate victim of Cain's execution, condemnation, and wrath. God, however, was his ultimate target. Cain's objective was to silence God's righteousness, thus (in his mind) establishing his own. Every murderer after Cain has attempted roughly the same thing. A murderer defies God's justice and exacts his own. Murderers are self-righteous people who think they are free to judge, condemn, and execute other human beings without God's consent. Nowhere is this fact more apparent than it is in the case of the persecution of the righteous.

Cain succeeded in killing Abel, his brother, but he failed to silence him because Abel was covered by the righteousness of God. Cain could no more silence the righteousness of God than you or I (or an atheist) can silence the sky since "the heavens are telling of the glory of God" (Ps. 19:1). There is nothing one can do to silence God's glorious handiwork. If men become silent concerning the glory of God, the stones will cry out (Luke 19:40; Hab. 2:9–14). Likewise, the righteousness of God is never silent. Thus Cain killed Abel, but he did not silence him. He also failed to silence God.

According to Genesis 4:10, the very lifeblood of Abel shouted audibly into heaven for justice. Abel's blood cried strongly enough to penetrate the gates of heaven, entering the very ears of God. Like a mother who instantly recognizes the cry of her own child in pain, God recognized the righteous cry of Abel's blood and responded immediately by calling Cain to account for murdering his brother. Not surprisingly, the blood of Abel is referred to in the rest of the Bible as "righteous" blood (Matt. 23:35; Heb. 11:4).

In Matthew 23, Jesus speaks of the murder of Abel by Cain, and he places this murder in the broader context of persecution. Jesus makes the point that Abel is the first of the righteous martyrs in the Old Testament and Zechariah the last.[4] Jesus links the blood of Abel with all the righteous blood shed on

---

4   In the ancient order of the Hebrew canon, the last book of the Old Testament Bible would have been 2 Chronicles. Thus, Zechariah would have been the last martyr in the Bible of Jesus's day.

the earth by such persecution. Thus, of course, God hears such blood crying out for justice. Like a morning alarm, innocent blood cries out that it is time to awaken holy justice.

The murder of Abel by Cain, then, is an adequate paradigm for us to begin putting together a biblical concept of persecution. Understanding persecution begins with understanding the difference between self-righteousness and God's righteousness. Self-righteousness, as we have seen, is found early in the Bible — as early as Genesis. Cain may best embody it, but he is not the first to display it. Did Adam and Eve not call the righteousness of God into question when they defiantly partook of the forbidden fruit? Cain dutifully followed his fallen family's line and sought to establish his own righteousness, turning away from the demands of God and turning to his own devices for ridding the world of anyone who would question his right ordering of human affairs.

Throughout the rest of our examination, we will see that the righteousness of God is an integral aspect of Christian persecution. God declared Abel righteous. Abel died on account of the righteousness of God. Thus, Abel should easily be viewed as the first martyr in the Bible — the first faithful witness who died on account of the righteousness of God. So back to the chapter's original question, Who is the first martyr? The answer is Abel. While Stephen is the first Christian martyr *after* Christ — and Christ himself is the first Christian martyr — Abel is the first in the Bible to die on account of the righteousness of God. Looking at the Bible in this way helps us to see three theological realities of persecution.

First, persecution originally occurred in defiance of God's righteousness. Second, though the immediate object of persecution was a human brother, the ultimate target of the persecution was God. Third, the presence of God is the root provocateur of persecution. If God had been silent, Cain would not have killed Abel. It was not the offering Abel presented that infuriated Cain; it was the fact that God accepted Abel's offering. Cain killed Abel because Cain rebelled against the righteous judgment of God — even after God warned him against succumbing to the murderous power of sin.

These three theological realities will be present throughout this book. They permeate the Old Testament, and they are only clarified further by the teachings of the New Testament. So let us next turn to the clear instructions of Jesus found in Matthew 5:10–12 concerning the dynamic of Christian persecution.

4

THE SERMON ON THE MOUNT:
"BLESSED ARE THE PERSECUTED"

*Blessed are you when others revile you and persecute
you and utter all kinds of evil against you falsely on
my account.*

(Matt. 5:11 ESV)

My wife and I have learned many things since moving to Southern California. One thing we've learned is that houses here cost a lot of money! Related to that, we've also discovered that we can, in fact, learn landscaping, plumbing, painting, carpentry — we've become jacks-of-all-trades. Only able to afford a fixer-upper, we're now heavily engaged in repairing and remodeling an older home.

Because of our newfound adventure in home ownership, we are constantly aware of other homes. We watch what others do — not to covet their possessions, but to learn from their successes. Recently, I have been paying closer attention to entryways. Grand entrances make a home either inviting or off-putting. An inviting entry carries the visitor into the foyer, where she will either desire to go further into the home or to turn around and run for the car. Entrances are important because they set the expectations for delving further into another's abode.

Matthew 5:1–10 serves as a grand entrance to the greatest sermon ever recorded: the Sermon on the Mount. The Sermon on the Mount has fascinated religious leaders around the world and through history from Augustine to

Gandhi, from Bonhoeffer to Martin Luther King Jr. If Clarence Bauman is exaggerating, he is doing so only slightly when he says, "The Sermon on the Mount is the most important and most controversial biblical text."[1] More recently, Charles Quarles has said, "No sermon ever preached has been more significant to the Christian church than the Sermon on the Mount."[2] This grand sermon is worthy of a spectacular entry, and Christ does not disappoint when he frames his great message with the Beatitudes. The Beatitudes (Matt. 5:3–10) form the entryway into the Sermon on the Mount with an emphasis on the poor (v. 3) and the persecuted (v. 10).[3]

Matthew 5:10–12: The Entryway to the Sermon

Both the poor and the persecuted are said to possess the kingdom of heaven. The first eight Beatitudes could stand alone as a complete unit, the way a porch might stand in front of a fine home in the Deep South. As mentioned, both the first and the last of these original eight Beatitudes promise the kingdom of heaven: "Blessed are the poor in spirit, for theirs is the kingdom of heaven. . . . Blessed are those who have been persecuted for the sake of righteousness, for theirs is the kingdom of heaven" (5:3, 10).

But a problem arises when the eight Beatitudes are viewed as the entryway into the sermon — a ninth Beatitude appears in verse 11: "Blessed are you when others revile you and persecute you and utter all kinds of evil against you falsely on my account" (ESV). What is the relationship between the original eight Beatitudes (which are framed by the kingdom) and the ninth Beatitude, which describes persecution as a blessing to the followers of Christ?

The simplest way to understand the tension between the eighth Beatitude (in v. 10) and the ninth Beatitude (in v. 11) is to return to our front porch

---

1   Clarence Bauman, *The Sermon on the Mount: The Modern Quest for Its Meaning* (Macon, GA: Mercer University Press, 1985), 3.

2   Charles Quarles, *Sermon on the Mount: Restoring Christ's Message to the Modern Church*, NAC Studies in Bible and Theology (Nashville: B & H Publishing Group, 2011), 1.

3   It is quite possible that the poor and the persecuted are intentionally linked. Often, the persecuted become the poor. My colleague, professor of Old Testament Dr. Jeff Mooney, pointed out this dynamic to me from the prophetic literature. Even today, the persecuted church in the Middle East has been brought to great poverty.

analogy and ask this question: is the front door of a home part of the porch or part of the main structure of the house itself? In some ways, it is both, isn't it? Likewise, the Sermon on the Mount is framed by its front porch — the eight Beatitudes (vv. 3–10); yet the ninth Beatitude (v. 11) is the door that sits on the hinges of the house. The porch is an invitation to the house, without giving full entry into it. The door, however, once it swings open on its hinges offers full entry into the home — and so it is with verse 11. It is the open door to the grandeur of Christ's Sermon on the Mount.

This interpretation, which views Matthew 5:11 as the doorway to entering more fully into the splendor of the sermon, rests on three hinges: *Christ*, *kingdom*, and *righteousness*. As would be the case with any door, these hinges both hold the door in place and ensure that the doorway functions to allow people to enter through it. Without these hinges in place, the door would serve little purpose, and any attempt at entry would require illegitimate force. With the three concepts of Christ, kingdom, and righteousness in place, the reader of Matthew's Gospel is poised to understand both the Sermon on the Mount and the reason Christ's followers will be persecuted. Let's consider, then, these three hinges in their proper turn.

Christ: The First Hinge

Christ is obviously the key to the sermon and to its interpretation. Matthew recorded these words of Jesus in such a way as to keep Christ the central focus of the sermon. The clear emphasis on Christ is evident in 5:11, where Christ states that his followers suffer persecution "*because of me.*" Why does persecution happen on account of Christ? Because the Christ who is teaching in chapters 5 through 7 is no mere teacher. He is something much more, as the first four chapters have already disclosed. From the very first verse of the Gospel, in fact, Matthew stacks up powerful terms pregnant with meaning in order to establish the identity of Jesus.[4]

In our English translations, Matthew's Gospel usually begins something

---

4 Dale Allison, *Studies in Matthew: Interpretation Past and Present* (Grand Rapids: Baker, 2005), 157–78, offers an introduction to the various ways the first eight words of Matthew have been translated, along with detailing the distinctions in various interpretations.

like "the book (or record) of genealogy." To us, that sounds more like a tracing of the family tree than it does anything else, but the original phrase probably links to the book of Genesis. As Grant Osborne notes, "The phrase in [Matthew] 1:1a is taken from Genesis 2:4; 5:1 (see Gen 6:1; 10:1; 11:10, 27; etc.), where it introduces genealogies or historical narrative and hints here that Jesus fulfills these events and brings a new beginning or new creation."[5] In other words, the Gospel opens with a hint that its central character — Jesus — is a divine figure bringing about God's new creation.

Obviously, that is quite a lot to draw from a single phrase in a single book, but once the entire picture is pieced together, it becomes clear that the Christ of Matthew is much more than a good Jewish teacher. He represents a new Genesis. As Stanley Hauerwas puts it, "*The book of the genesis of Jesus Christ* is not a modest beginning. Matthew starts by suggesting that the genealogy of this man Jesus requires our revisiting the very beginning of God's creative acts."[6]

The other four titles in Matthew 1:1 are equally charged with cosmic implications. So the English name "Jesus" (Greek *Iesou*) has its own Old Testament background. Scholars have long noted that the English name "Jesus" is equivalent to the Hebrew name "Joshua." Joshua was a giant figure in the history of Israel, and he led Israel into the Promised Land and the conquest of Canaan after the death of Moses.

In Matthew 1:1, the name "Jesus" does not stand alone; it is coupled with "Christ." The first Greek phrase could be translated, "the book of the Genesis of Jesus Christ." While the titles "Jesus Christ" do stand together, they should not be confused with the manner in which one would be named in English. "Jesus Christ" (two titles) is not the same as "John Smith" (a first name with a surname). "Jesus" and "Christ" are titles, the first meaning "deliverer," the second meaning "anointed one." So Jesus is rightly viewed as the one anointed by God to bring deliverance to his people. In fact, Matthew 1:21 says precisely that "she [Mary] will bear a son, and you shall call his name Jesus, for he will save his people from their sins" (ESV). Thus, even though Matthew links the two titles together, by verse 21, he makes clear his intent

---

5 Grant Osborne, *Matthew*, Zondervan Exegetical Commentary on the New Testament (Grand Rapids: Zondervan, 2010), 61–62.

6 Stanley Hauerwas, *Matthew*, Brazos Theological Commentary on the Bible (Grand Rapids: Brazos, 2006), 23. Original quote-marks changed here to italics for readability.

to give the title "Jesus" its full significance — Jesus is a deliverer like Joshua sent from God.

With allusions to Genesis and to Joshua, Matthew demonstrates an uncanny knack for loading terms with historical and theological significance. The same is true for the next term in the opening verse: Christ (Greek *Christou*). As noted, this term means "anointed one." In the Hebrew mindset, the concept of anointing belonged to the Messiah. In effect, Matthew lets the reader know from the very first line of the first verse of his Gospel that Jesus is in fact the long hoped-for Christ.

The implications of the Messiah having come are staggering both for Rome and for the people of God. As one scholar has shown, the term "Christ" signals the end of the status quo and "the establishment of God's very different world."[7] Matthew's announcement that the Messiah had come in Jesus Christ is no small bit of news; it would change all of history, as it signaled the establishment of a new kingdom and ushered in a future hope of an eternally different world. And, I should add, the ushering in of a new era necessarily creates tension with those who have a vested interest in maintaining the old one.

Much like the concepts built into the term "Christ," so, too, Matthew's use of the next phrase — "son of David" — is ripe with historical meaning. David was the quintessential king of the Old Testament. David (unlike Saul) was the king of the tribe of Judah (Gen. 49:10), the king after God's own choosing — not the one demanded by popular vote (Acts 13:22). The highpoint of Israel's history was rooted in the kingship of David (2 Sam. 7). So when earthly rulers heard that the "son of David" had come, they obviously perceived a threat to their own power. Herod understood the threat and demanded this "son of David" be put to death (Matt. 2:16). Matthew, however, portrayed Jesus as the rightful heir to the throne of Israel. In short, Matthew announced that God's king — and thus God's kingdom — had arrived in this Jesus Christ. *Christ's arrival caused no small tension in the first century.*

Finally, the fifth title of Jesus in Matthew 1:1 reflects the fulfillment of covenant promises for God's people. Jesus is referred to as the "son of Abraham."

---

7   Warren Carter, "Matthean Christology in Roman Imperial Key: Matthew 1:1," in *The Gospel of Matthew in Its Roman Imperial Context*, ed. John Riches and David Sim, JSNTSup 276 (London: T & T Clark, 2005), 157. This is an academic book with which evangelicals will disagree on several matters.

Leon Morris captures the significance of calling Jesus the son of Abraham when he says, "It was Abraham with whom God made the covenant that set Israel apart in a special sense as the people of God. . . . All Israelites took pride in being descendants of the great patriarch, and the Christians were especially fond of him as the classic example of one who believed."[8] With the inclusion of Abraham, Matthew is encapsulating the fulfillment of Israel's history within the life of this single person Jesus Christ.

The Old Testament story reaches its high-water mark with the arrival of Jesus, who flooded the world with the righteousness of God. From the very beginning of Matthew's Gospel, Jesus has been presented as no trivial being. Thus, when Jesus proclaims the message of the Sermon on the Mount, he does so as God, shaping his own people for his kingdom. Understanding this fact about Jesus is the first hinge that opens the door to the fuller understanding of why (according to the Sermon on the Mount) Christians must face persecution.

Kingdom: The Second Hinge

The second hinge is that of Christ's kingdom. King and kingdom go together even more closely than a hand goes with a glove. To be a king is to have a kingdom, and vice versa. With the piling on of all these power-laden titles, Matthew expects the reader of the Sermon on the Mount to understand the authority of Christ. Christ is king! When Christ goes up to the mountain to teach (5:1–2), he speaks like God spoke from Mt. Sinai, which is to say, he speaks as one with the authority of God.

Consider all that has been said of Christ in chapters 1 through 4. In Matthew 1:23, this Son of David is to be called "Immanuel," which is "God with us." Here, Matthew connects the heavenly kingdom with earthly men. When the magi from the East heard about it, they came to Jerusalem with the question, "Where is He who has been born *King of the Jews*?" (Matt. 2:2; emphasis mine). This king of the Jews turned out to be the ruler from Bethlehem, spoken of by the prophet Micah (Micah 5:2; see Matt. 2:6). Herod,

---

8   Leon Morris, *The Gospel According to Matthew,* The Pillar New Testament Commentary (Grand Rapids: Eerdmans, 1992), 20.

who occupied the office of king, responded to the birth of this so-called child-king by ordering his destruction. (It is no small threat for a king to have in his kingdom another referred to by that same title.) Under the threat of death, the child who would be king was ushered into Egypt for safety until the death of Herod.[9] Then at the end of chapter 2, this child-king returned.

In chapter 3, Matthew records John the Baptist preaching repentance at the arrival of the kingdom of heaven, hinting that the king himself was close at hand and far greater than him. Indeed, John preached from Isaiah that the time had come to fulfill all righteousness. Significantly, John then baptized the king "to fulfill all righteousness" (v. 15). The reader will find out later (21:32) that the *way* of Jesus's preaching and work of John the Baptist was, in fact, the *way* of righteousness. And the king himself, in Matthew 4:17, is portrayed as preaching, "Repent, for the kingdom of heaven is at hand." Jesus, the preaching king in chapter 4, chose disciples for himself (presumably against Jewish cultural norms, which would have expected the disciples to choose their teacher).[10] Christ then demonstrated his authority over diseases, pains, demoniacs, and paralytics through his miraculous healings, all the while preaching "the gospel of the kingdom" (4:23).

Thus, by the time the reader gets to chapter 5 of Matthew, he is, to say the least, not completely unaware of the kingship authority claimed for and by Jesus — an authority further reaffirmed by the response to the Sermon on the Mount. The original audience was not startled at the high ethical demands Jesus proposed. They were not primarily amazed by his claim that the kingdom belonged to those whose righteousness exceeded that of the scribes and the Pharisees. Rather, the original crowd was astonished because Christ taught as one having his own authority (7:29). Christ speaks in Matthew from his own mouth with the authority of God about the kingdom of heaven. Christ speaks as the king of heaven and earth (see 28:18–20). Entry into the Sermon on the Mount, then, is further clarified by realizing Christ is speaking about the kingdom of heaven with sovereign authority as God's king.

---

9 Ulrich Luz, *Matthew 1–7*, rev. ed., Heremenia (Minneapolis: Fortress, 2007), 152–55, offers an excursus in table form that suggests a thematic background of "the persecuted and rescued royal child" for Matthew 1:18–2:23.

10 See Robert Gundry, *Matthew: A Commentary on His Handbook for a Mixed Church Under Persecution*, 2nd ed. (Grand Rapids: Eerdmans, 1994), 62.

Righteousness: The Final Hinge

We've explored the concepts of *Christ* and *kingdom* as they are used in the Sermon on the Mount. *Righteousness* is the third hinge that opens the door to understanding Christ's sermon. Though Matthew doesn't mention the idea of righteousness much in chapters 1–4, his use of it in 3:15 is significant. There (as noted above) Christ underwent the baptism of John in order "to fulfill all righteousness." Christ fulfills all righteousness because he is established by God as the true king of heaven and earth (see 21:32; 28:19). Fittingly, then, righteousness — beginning with the baptism of John — pervades Christ's kingdom.

Though righteousness is spoken of only once in chapters 1–4, it is a central concept in the Sermon on the Mount, where it is discussed five times in this relatively short message:

5:6 — "Blessed are those who hunger and thirst for righteousness, for they shall be satisfied."

5:10 — "Blessed are those who have been persecuted for the sake of righteousness, for theirs is the kingdom of heaven."

5:20 — "For I say to you that unless your righteousness surpasses that of the scribes and Pharisees, you will not enter the kingdom of heaven."

6:1 — "Beware of practicing your righteousness before men to be noticed by them; otherwise you have no reward with your Father who is in heaven."

6:33 — "But seek first His kingdom and His righteousness, and all these things will be added to you."

The pervasive manner in which righteousness fills the kingdom is displayed in these six verses. Many books and articles explore the nature of righteousness in Matthew. For years, most scholars interpreted these verses as a kind of demand — as something the followers of Christ were bound to do in order to prove themselves to be part of the kingdom. There is no doubt that righteousness is related to the kingdom of heaven. But how?

Recently, scholars have begun questioning the notion that righteousness in these verses must be about an ethical demand (or moral conduct). Instead, they view the righteousness of these verses as belonging to Jesus himself. It seems to me that righteousness in the Sermon on the Mount is better explained by relating it primarily to Jesus Christ and the in-breaking of the kingdom of heaven rather than to the righteous behavior of the followers of Jesus. Consider, for example, the difference this would make in the interpretation of Matthew 5:20.

Under the more popular scheme, righteousness in 5:20 would be viewed as that which belonged to the followers of Jesus. The verse would mean that no one can hope to enter the kingdom of heaven until their own righteousness reaches a level that is greater than the righteousness practiced by the Pharisees. But how could a Christian hope to "out-Pharisee" the Pharisees? Who would want heaven to depend on whether one's righteous deeds were superior to those of the religious leaders of Jesus's day? More important, is this really what Jesus is demanding?

A number of problems arise if this is what Jesus has in view (not the least of which is the great tension of holding such a position while avoiding a works-based righteousness for salvation). For our study of persecution, however, a serious problem surfaces when we ask why the disciples, who are striving to excel the Pharisees in righteousness (5:20), would end up being persecuted by those Pharisees on the basis of righteousness (5:10). Wouldn't the Pharisees instead applaud their attempts to mimic them?

Is Jesus really calling his followers to be better Pharisees? This interpretation appears unlikely — especially by the time the reader gets to 23:25: "Woe to you, scribes and Pharisees, hypocrites! For you clean the outside of the cup and of the dish, but inside they are full of robbery and self-indulgence." It seems much better to understand the righteousness of 5:20 (and 5:10 for that matter) to refer not to the righteousness of the disciples per se but to the righteousness of Christ on display through them. Doesn't it make sense to say that the kingdom of heaven belongs to those who are the partakers of the righteousness of Christ? Those who have been given the kingdom filled with the righteousness of God are the ones who have a righteousness that exceeds that of the scribes and the Pharisees. Jesus is not telling his followers in 5:20 that they must do better than the Pharisees. He is not calling them to perfect legalism (or a less-perfect hypocrisy). He is calling them to himself. Jesus's own righteousness is the righteousness that exceeds that of the scribes and the Pharisees and everyone else. Our Lord's point in making this statement is to assure us that the kingdom of heaven is an impossibility apart from him — even the Pharisees won't make it on their own righteousness.

This understanding of righteousness (belonging to Jesus, who is God incarnate) completes the three hinges that open the door to understanding the Sermon on the Mount more fully, which is integral to recognizing why Jesus is teaching his followers to expect persecution. So with better awareness now of the three hinges — Christ, kingdom, and righteousness — let's enter into Christ's teaching in the Sermon on the Mount and find out why his followers are persecuted.

The Sermon on the Mount and Christian Persecution

So far in this chapter, we have reviewed quite a bit of material from Matthew's Gospel. It's time to consolidate it and come to a conclusion about the essence of the Sermon on the Mount. *Essentially, the Sermon on the Mount is a guidebook for those who follow Jesus Christ.* While it is true, generally, that Christ addressed a multitude of people in this sermon, he instructed his disciples specifically in the way of righteousness. Thus, Matthew 5:1 states that Jesus saw the crowds of people, but he spoke specifically to his disciples who had come near to him to listen to the sermon. One might think of the context of Christ's sermon as being roughly equivalent to many sermons in our own day — sermons that recognize that nonbelievers are in the audience, even while their content is primarily aimed at instructing believers in the way of Christ.

So what guidance is Christ offering his followers in this sermon? Basically, as noted above, he is calling his followers to himself. He is teaching as one having authority from God, and he is telling them to follow him because he is giving them the kingdom of heaven. Thus, the bulk of the instruction is clarifying what it means to be citizens of the kingdom of heaven. What does Christ say it means to be kingdom people?

- It means being salt and light in a dark and fallen world (5:13–16).
- It means disciples of Christ (not Pharisees) are actually on the side of the law because they are faithful to Christ, the law-fulfiller (5:17–19).

- It means the kingdom belongs to Christ and his people (5:20).
- It means the disciples demonstrate the righteousness of God when they obey the commands of Christ (5:21–48). Whatever religious consensus might say, the disciples display God's righteousness when they do what Christ demands.
- It means the disciples prove that their citizenship is in heaven and not on earth because they seek to please the Father in heaven — not to impress religious leaders and others on earth (6:1–8).
- It means the disciples pray daily to advance the kingdom of heaven and live — as their heavenly Father lives — with a heart toward forgiving others (6:9–15).
- It means the disciples fast for what they pray daily — that God's kingdom would come and his will be done (6:16–18).
- It means the disciples need not be controlled by earthly treasures, for they have the kingdom of heaven. Thus, they store their treasures in heaven (6:20) and learn not to be anxious about lacking materially while on earth (6:25–34).
- It means disciples aren't haughty and self–righteous; thus, they do not sit in judgment over others (7:1–6).
- It means disciples love God, commune with him, and do good to others in his name (7:7–12).
- It means disciples will be a minority who walk in a narrow way that is not popular — even in a religious culture (7:13–14).
- It means disciples will have discernment, being able to distinguish between what is good and what is bad — between those who bear good fruit and those who bear the fruit of unrighteousness (7:15–23).
- It means those who have Christ as their foundation cannot be shaken even if the rain and wind and floods (of persecution?) come against them. Kingdom people do not depend on their own righteousness; they rest in the righteousness of Christ, which they have received in the kingdom of heaven. All those outside the kingdom will ultimately fall because their foundation was something other than the Christ of Matthew's Gospel (7:24–27).

Little wonder when we read the sermon this way that those who first heard it were amazed that Jesus made himself out to be the king of heaven and earth

(7:28–29)! Christ himself is the only way of righteousness. The kingdom of heaven belongs to him and to his disciples to whom he gives it. His disciples ought, therefore, to live as citizens of a heavenly kingdom: to seek first his kingdom and his righteousness.

Persecution: Christ, Kingdom, and Righteousness

So these three key concepts — Christ, kingdom, and righteousness — help explain the entire sermon. But how do they help explain Christian persecution? Recall that the Sermon on the Mount is framed by the Beatitudes. The Beatitudes proclaim that the kingdom of heaven belongs to the poor and the persecuted (5:3, 10). The Beatitudes act as a front porch to the Sermon on the Mount. The three hinges open the door to the sermon. But where is the door? I think the door is found in Matthew 5:11–12: "Blessed are you when people insult you and persecute you, and falsely say all kinds of evil against you because of Me. Rejoice and be glad, for your reward in heaven is great, for in the same way they persecuted the prophets who were before you."

In Matthew 5:11–12, Jesus changes his tone from the general sense in which he speaks the blessings of the first eight Beatitudes to the very specific application to his disciples in verse 11. In the first eight Beatitudes, Jesus says, "Blessed are the poor. . . . Blessed are those who mourn. . . . Blessed are the gentle. . . . Blessed are the merciful . . . ," but in verse 11, Jesus says quite directly to his disciples: "Blessed are you when people insult you and persecute you." The primary focus of the sermon changes in this verse to direct address. The disciples must learn the way of Jesus's kingdom, which will include persecution.

In the list of bullet points above, we learned what it means for Jesus's disciples to be kingdom people. Being kingdom people means displaying God's righteousness. In 5:11, we see that living in righteousness also means facing persecution just like the prophets. The dynamic hangs together in this way: Jesus Christ establishes the kingdom of heaven on earth (already begun, but not yet completed); he calls people to himself, gives them a new life, and makes them citizens of this heavenly kingdom; Jesus tells his followers what this new life means, and he instructs them on how to live in the light of this glorious new reality; he gives the kingdom, and then he commands its citizens to follow his way of righteousness.

In many ways, this pattern is reflected in the Old Testament. God redeemed his people, gave them the Promised Land, and then commanded them to follow the way of righteousness in it. We see this same pattern reflected often in everyday life.

Consider this example from my days in pastoral ministry. I regularly spent time in hospitals, visiting those sick and in need of healing. In one particular hospital, the expectation was clear that everyone had a responsibility to fight germs. The floors were always spotless. The walls and ceilings were always clean and freshly painted. Hand-sanitizing dispensers were at every entrance, in every hallway, and in every room (two, in fact) so that doctors, nurses, orderlies, and visitors alike could keep their hands germfree.

In addition to ensuring that all hands were sanitized, this hospital also made certain that the laboratory was accessible only to lab technicians and the new baby nursery only to authorized doctors and nurses; that the surgery room was open to authorized personnel only; that the roof could be accessed exclusively by the maintenance men with the keys to the lock. Why all these rules and regulations? Why all of the commandments like "do not enter," or "wash hands thoroughly"? The answer is a kind of righteousness.

Just as the righteousness of God demanded certain actions from Israel in the Promised Land, so too the righteousness of the hospital administrators sets forth certain expectations for the people in the hospital's dominion. The administrators first hire their employees, then teach them how to act in accordance with hospital righteousness. God calls his people to his kingdom, and then he instructs them to act according to the calling. In ancient Israel, one primary function of the king was to execute God's righteousness. The king was supposed to study the Word of God and hold forth the expectation of what it meant to be a member of the kingdom of Israel. The author of 2 Samuel, for example, says that David reigned over all Israel and administered justice and righteousness for all his people (8:15). That was a primary aspect of the king's function (see Deut. 17). The pattern is clear. Those with authority are expected to use their authority to administer justice. They establish righteousness in their domains — whether the domain is a regional hospital or the nation of Israel.

In the Sermon on the Mount, Christ is calling his people to follow the way of righteousness in his kingdom. In the kingdom, righteousness is neither created nor increased by the individual citizen. It is displayed. The source is higher than any one individual. Righteousness comes from above. Christ as king is himself righteous. His righteousness is executed in his will. His will is reflected in his commands and his ordering of the events and purposes of his kingdom. His commands are righteous because they reflect God's nature. Ultimately, kingdom citizens obey kingdom demands because they know, trust, and love the God who has given those commands.

When entering a hospital, the "Do Not Enter" signs need to be obeyed. The visitor ought to use hand sanitizer before and after holding a patient's hand. Why? Because such things are good. They are rightly expected in a hospital.

Likewise, when sinners enter God's creation, they too ought to obey the "Do Not Enter" signs. They too ought to have clean hands. However, people do not naturally obey God because people by nature are unrighteous. Happily, the miracle of Jesus and the gospel is that God calls unrighteous people to himself. He cleanses through the atoning work of Christ and makes people new in the regenerating work of the Holy Spirit. God then commands his people to walk in the narrow way of righteousness — which is the way that reflects his character, his will, and his commands. Because God is righteous, his ways are righteous. When God's people understand this dynamic, they themselves display the righteousness of God. To be more precise, they display the righteousness of God in Jesus Christ (call it Jesus-righteousness).[11]

The essence of this righteousness dynamic is supported by Jesus's teaching in Matthew 5:10–12. In verse 10, Jesus says those who are persecuted on account of righteousness are the blessed people of the kingdom. In verse 11, Jesus says to his disciples specifically that they are blessed when others persecute them on account of him. Jesus and righteousness go together. Followers of Jesus are persecuted on account of righteousness, and they are persecuted on account of Jesus. The two are interconnected because righteousness — though it is manifested by the disciples — belongs ultimately to

---

11   The term "Jesus-Righteousness" is used by Roland Deines in his persuasive essay, "Not the Law but the Messiah: Law and Righteousness in the Gospel of Matthew — An Ongoing Debate," in *Built Upon the Rock: Studies in the Gospel of Matthew*, ed. Daniel M. Gurtner and John Nolland (Grand Rapids: Eerdmans, 2008). This essay from Deines has influenced greatly my interpretation of Matthew and the Sermon on the Mount.

Jesus himself. When the disciples suffer persecution, they suffer it only as the immediate, most convenient objects. The ultimate target of persecution's wrath is Jesus. The real fuel behind the fire of persecution is rebellion against Christ. Thus, in verse 11, Jesus says the disciples' persecution is on account of him. Surely, the disciples suffer, but the persecutor is really fighting against Jesus (see Acts 9:3–5).

Conclusion

Jesus taught his followers that they would suffer persecution on account of him. The reasoning, as we have seen, is clear enough. Jesus is not merely a good teacher. He is God's king. His work accomplishes God's eternal, kingdom purposes on earth. His people understand the eternal stakes and gladly obey him. As they obey, they display his salvation, his righteousness, and his sovereign authority. The unbelieving mind, on the other hand, desires no king from heaven with eternal dominion. So Herod slaughtered all suspects resembling Jesus (2:16); the soldiers, the thieves, the religious leaders, and many spectators openly mocked him at his crucifixion (Matt. 27). The world was opposed to Jesus in the first century, and the world opposes him still.

Christ's followers display his righteousness. Those who love him are those who have been saved, redeemed, reconciled — those who have been given the kingdom. They represent the righteousness of God in the salvation of sinners. They know the king of heaven and earth, and they are charged by him to tell the rest of the world about Christ. Not surprisingly, the next to the last thing Christ tells his disciples in Matthew's Gospel is this: "All authority has been given to Me in heaven and on earth. Go therefore and make disciples of all the nations, baptizing them in the name of the Father and the Son and the Holy Spirit, teaching them to observe all that I commanded you" (28:18–20a). The weight of this command, which we call the Great Commission, is magnificent. Christ claims kingship authority over Saudi Arabia, Jerusalem, Tibet, and India. He charges his own disciples to teach people everywhere to obey what he has commanded. And the result of such actions will often be persecution. The world today (as in the first century) is not always eager to hear a word from God — especially if that word contradicts the desires of fleshly appetites. No wonder Christ was executed! And little wonder that his people suffer many forms of persecution.

Christ promises to remain present with his people. The next to the last thing Christ says in Matthew's Gospel is to make disciples of all the earth. The last thing he offers his followers is this promise: "Lo, I am with you always, even to the end of the age."

What a great promise Christ offers his people! Knowing his people would face opposition as they carried out his kingdom mandate to disciple the earth, Christ promises his presence with his people. Jesus teaches his followers (10:16–31) that they will be sent out as sheep in the midst of wolves. But he then encourages them not to worry about what to say when the persecutors demand that they give some account of their insubordination against the world's agenda. Christ tells them that his Spirit will speak through them (10:20). Christ teaches his followers to proclaim his truth from the rooftops (10:27) and never shrink back in fear because their souls will remain safe with him even if their bodies are killed (10:28–31). What more does the follower of Christ need in tumultuous times than to know his Lord is with him? Christ promises himself to his people forever.

Persecution happens to God's people because Christ is present with them (5:11). Christ's righteousness is the root cause of the aggravation that leads to the persecution of Christ's people. Though Christ is the reason his followers are persecuted, he also is the reward: "Blessed are you when people insult you and persecute you, and falsely say all kinds of evil against you because of Me. Rejoice and be glad, for your reward in heaven is great." Because Christ is present with his kingdom people, persecution is not a curse. It is a sign of God's blessing. To understand better the relation between Christ, persecution, and reward, we turn our attention in the following chapter to Mark's Gospel and the promise of persecution related to eternal life.

5

THE GOSPEL OF MARK:
THE HIGH COST OF FOLLOWING JESUS

For whoever wishes to save his life will lose it, but whoever loses his life for My sake and the gospel's will save it.
(Mark 8:35)

In 2009, in a television segment, comedian Stephen Colbert invited New Testament scholar (and critic) Bart Ehrman to spar over the nature of Jesus Christ. Ehrman had just published a book, *Jesus Interrupted*, in which he argued against the deity of Christ. According to Ehrman, the first three Gospels (Matthew, Mark, Luke) never present Jesus claiming to be God, while the fourth Gospel, John, does. In the previous chapter, we saw clearly that Matthew does present Jesus claiming to be the sovereign of heaven and earth, God's anointed king and ruler. Rather than arguing with Ehrman about the specific content found in Matthew, Colbert used a more subtle strategy.

Colbert invited Ehrman to consider a parable. In the parable, four blind men walking through the jungle inadvertently fall into a pit. Once in the pit, the four discovered they were not alone. A very large, living creature was in the pit with them. The creature turned out to be an elephant, but because the elephant was much larger than any of the blind men, each man could only describe a part of its size and shape. When pieced together, the testimonies of the four men allowed them to understand that the animal in the pit was an elephant. Likewise, Colbert noted, the four Gospels when taken together portray Jesus consistently as God incarnate, even while each Gospel independently highlights unique aspects of Jesus and his ministry.

As in the Gospel of Matthew, so too in the Gospel of Mark, Jesus Christ is portrayed as having come from heaven with the authority of God. So Jesus is seen preaching, "The kingdom of God is at hand; repent and believe in the gospel" (1:15b ESV). Despite Ehrman's insinuations to the contrary, Jesus is clearly pictured as the Son of God throughout Mark's Gospel. In no less than five places, Jesus is referred to as the Son of God (1:1; 1:11; 3:11, 9:7; 15:39). As Colbert pointed out humorously to Ehrman, "The son of a duck is a duck, and the Son of God is God." The same anointed Messiah appears in both Matthew and Mark — even if different aspects of his ministry are emphasized by the two Gospel writers.

The arrival of Jesus as God incarnate surprised Mark's readers just as it surprised Matthew's readers. Jesus consistently caught his hearers off guard: "And they were astonished at his teaching, for he taught them as one who had authority, and not as the scribes" (1:22 ESV).

Jesus taught with such authority that even the spirits obeyed him (1:27). The authority of Jesus was plainly manifested over both earthly powers like diseases and over the demonic realm (1:34). Throughout this Gospel, Jesus demonstrated his authority to forgive sins (2:7), to rule the Sabbath (2:28), and to overpower death (5:42). In short, Mark's Gospel unfolds what is briefly stated in its first verse: Jesus Christ is the Son of God. Therefore, he is able to heal the sick, give sight to the blind, cause the deaf to hear, make the lame to walk, and — for all who believe — accomplish the impossible task of salvation, granting entry into the kingdom of God. The scribes ask, "Who can forgive sins but God alone?" (2:7). Jesus answers by not only offering forgiveness of sins but by telling a lame man to get up and walk in the presence of these doubting scribes. Jesus is pictured consistently in both Matthew and Mark as more than a teacher, more than an earthly king.

While Matthew and Mark approach their Gospels in different ways, they each ultimately describe the same Messiah — Jesus Christ, the divine ruler who executes the plan and purposes of God. Consequently, in Mark's Gospel, just as in Matthew, Jesus tells his followers to expect persecution. The question we are exploring in this chapter, then, is whether Jesus speaks differently about persecution in Mark. According to this Gospel, how does Jesus prepare his followers for expecting to suffer persecution?

Since a martyr is a Christian who endures persecution unto death, martyrdom and persecution are closely linked. Many scholars have noted that persecution (and martyrdom) plays a significant role in Mark. Almost one hundred years ago, Donald Riddle, professor of New Testament at the University of Chicago Divinity School, wrote a significant article on the martyr motif in Mark. Since the time of this article, scholars have noted the prominence of the persecution theme in this Gospel.[1] A number of these scholars have concluded that the Gospel must have been intended for an audience suffering under persecution. As one New Testament scholar says, "There can be little doubt that Mark finds himself and his church in the throes of a persecution severely testing the survival capacity of the faith."[2]

Most of Markan scholarship explores whether Mark's audience was suffering persecution when he wrote his Gospel. My own contention is that we may never know for sure who the first readers of the Gospel were. Regardless of whether the original audience was suffering persecution, Mark's Gospel offers important instructions to the followers of Christ about persecution. This chapter, in fact, demonstrates that the persecution against Christ's followers (in the past and continually present) connects directly to Christ himself in a manner consistent with Matthew. To accomplish this aim, we must first explore the strongest evidence that favors the view that Mark's Gospel was written to Christians suffering persecution. Out of this exploration will emerge a portrait of a persecution that, as the second portion of the chapter shows, implies that all faithful followers of Jesus can expect persecution as a result of belonging to Christ.

Martyrdom and the First Readers of Mark's Gospel

We begin our exploration of evidence in 10:29–30:

> Jesus said, "Truly, I say to you, there is no one who has left house or brothers or sisters or mother or father or children or lands for my sake

---

1 Donald W. Riddle, "The Martyr Motif in the Gospel According to Mark," *The Journal of Religion* 4 (1924): 397–410.

2 Theodore J. Weeden, *Mark: Traditions in Conflict* (Philadelphia: Fortress, 1971), 82.

and for the gospel, who will not receive a hundredfold now in this time, houses and brothers and sisters and mothers and children and lands, *with persecutions,* and in the age to come eternal life." (ESV; emphasis mine)

In contrast to the parallel passages of Matthew 19:29 and Luke 18:30, Mark adds "with persecutions" to the section that speaks of reward for those who suffer on behalf of Christ. The question is why Mark's Gospel adds this phrase. Scholars, preachers, and theologians differ. Some think that early Christians added the saying to what Mark originally wrote to offer a sober reminder to other Christians that following Christ would not always be easy. Other scholars think that Mark himself added the phrase even though Jesus might never have said it. Still others reject the saying outright as an artificial addition by someone after Mark. Most evangelical scholars believe that Jesus did say "with persecutions" and further believe Mark kept the phrase in his Gospel because he felt that his audience needed to be encouraged about their suffering. This conclusion, however, is not ironclad proof of Mark's intentions. Are we sure Mark's audience was already suffering persecution?

Because the Gospel of Mark offers so few clues about its sources and the purpose for which it was written, scholars frequently talk about the difficulty of reconstructing this Gospel. Robert Stein asks, "How then are we to determine what the sources which were available to Mark were like?"[3] He points out that Mark's unique writing style helps to identify what his original material is, but, in the end, he says, "The difficulty of ascertaining the pre-Markan tradition is not to be minimized."[4] So the exact origin of the phrase "with persecutions" remains contested and uncertain. Therefore, the claim that it is an addition necessary to address the issues of a persecuted audience is at minimum not 100 percent certain.

Scholars are right to note that the phrase "with persecutions" might mean that Mark's original audience was suffering persecution. However, saying what a phrase *might* mean is not the same as saying what it *must* mean. It seems just as probable to conclude that the phrase does not mean that the context of Mark's readers was one of persecution. After all, the phrase in

---

3 Robert Stein, "The Proper Methodology for Ascertaining a Markan Redaction History," in *The Composition of Mark's Gospel: Selected Studies from Novum Testamentum,* ed. David E. Orton (Leiden: Brill, 1999), 35.

4 Stein, "The Proper Methodology," 39.

Mark 10:30 is written in the form of direct speech from the mouth of Jesus speaking to his disciples in response to a comment from Peter. Mark has painted a scene in which the disciples question how anyone can be saved, and Jesus answers with instruction on the blessings of salvation. Jesus includes "with persecutions" in this list of blessings.

As the scene is described, the original audience consists of the inquisitive followers of Christ. Most immediately, then, the persecutions do not apply to this original literary audience (the disciples). The disciples did not suffer persecutions until after Christ's resurrection. Christ's saying to Peter that blessings will come "with persecutions" hints that the time in question had its origins as far back as this very conversation and is enduring beyond Christ's resurrection.

One could say that this is the scholars' very point: the author of the Gospel inserted this phrase into the mouth of Jesus speaking to his followers so that the readers of Mark's Gospel would realize that God rewards those who suffer with Jesus. In this way of adding the phrase, the author would be offering encouragement to those disciples who follow Jesus through times of persecution. Yet, as noted, the certainty of the addition of this phrase has not been established. Further, most evangelicals would be uncomfortable with the idea of a biblical writer adding phrases to the sermons of Jesus. If Mark added the phrase for this purpose, the question could well have been raised by the original readers whether Jesus actually said "with persecutions." Mark's Gospel was most likely written before the death of all the apostles. If the writer of Mark had contrived the entire story (or just the line on persecution), then it seems that someone would have questioned it. After all, if we were to hear someone claim that Richard Nixon once promised his staff that the Democratic Party would attempt to assassinate him, we would be quick to investigate and dispute the person's claim. Even more, we would have a visceral reaction to alert us to the dubious nature of the claim. Yet the distance between our time and the time of Richard Nixon is most likely greater than the distance between Jesus's ministry and the writing of Mark.[5]

---

5 This statement would allow a possible date for Mark as late as the middle 60s, only thirty-five years or so after the death of Jesus as opposed to the forty-one years that have passed (as of this writing) since Nixon's resignation from office in 1974. For dating Mark, see D. A. Carson, Douglas J. Moo, and Leon Morris, *An Introduction to the New Testament* (Grand Rapids: Zondervan, 1992), 99, who argue for a date in the middle 50s.

It is possible that some of Mark's original audience had met Jesus. In addition, Peter and John both were still probably alive as Mark's Gospel was making its rounds throughout the Roman Empire. If evidence existed that Christ had never spoken this phrase, then there would be little encouragement for the Christians receiving the Gospel. Additionally, if the original recipients of Mark thought he made something up and added it to the Gospel, they may also have had doubts about embracing other teachings in the Gospel as authentic. If Christ did not actually teach his original followers that rewards would come "with persecutions," then why should Mark's audience be comforted by the writer's attempt to say that he did? If the writer of Mark were to delude his readers on this point, then might he not also have deluded them on other points in the Gospel? The addition, then, rather than comforting the readers, might have ended up discrediting the Gospel. One is left to wonder whether such an addition would actually have encouraged the persecuted. The idea of an addition seems both implausible and inefficient. If we can doubt that Mark inserted the phrase in order to encourage an audience suffering persecution, then we might also doubt whether Mark's first audience was undergoing persecution.

Considering Mark 10:30, Craig Evans concludes, "In the time of the evangelist Mark and his community, the phrase 'with persecutions' may have reflected the harsh persecutions inflicted on Christians by Nero following the disastrous fire that destroyed half of the city of Rome. But the prophecy may very well derive from Jesus himself and reflect his expectations of struggle and violent opposition before the kingdom of God finally obliterates evil."[6] Evans makes the reasonable point that Mark's audience might have been in a time of persecution, but also might not have been. The phrase "with persecutions" goes back to the original preaching of Jesus and, as Evans notes, is connected with the kingdom.

I pause here in case some readers are wondering why this book about persecution just spent several pages countering the claim that Mark's original audience was suffering persecution. As odd as it may seem, this clarifying challenge is necessary. When persecution does come, the believer needs to know with fearless certainty what Christ has said about it. We must be care-

---

6   Craig A. Evans, *Mark 8:27–16:20*, Word Biblical Commentary (Nashville: Thomas Nelson, 2001), 103.

ful to build our case from the Scriptures, not from contextual speculation. So given the uncertainty of whether Mark's readers were persecuted, and given the probability that the phrase "with persecutions" hearkens back to Christ himself, the point of 10:30 is best interpreted to mean that persecutions may come against the Christian at any time, from "now in this time" until "the age to come."

Using the framework of 10:30, the saying "the age to come" refers to all of the time from Christ's original coming to the coming age after his return. The persecutions in question might have occurred at the time of Mark's original readers, or they might have occurred before the time of Mark's audience, or they might have occurred after the original audience. The persecutions are pictured as *perpetual potentialities* characterizing the present age. The term "perpetual" here, as in its botanical use to describe plants that flower seasonally, refers to a "seasonal flowering" for a time but not always occurring. One scholar sums up the idea this way: "The persecutions are represented as being characteristic for the time preceding the coming aeon. . . . Anything preceding that aeon therefore belongs to the time characterized by persecutions and not only to the time during which the book was written."[7] Suffering persecution is always possible for Christians prior to Christ's return according to 10:30. Persecution may come with the blessing of belonging to Christ.

Mark 13

What else does Mark say about Jesus and persecution? Mark 13 includes a number of direct references to persecution. In verse 9, Jesus tells the disciples to "be on your guard"[8] because they will be called before councils, will be beaten, and will stand before governors and kings for Christ's sake. Verse 11 promises the followers of Christ that they will receive a word from the Spirit when they are most anxious about what to say in defense at their trials. Verse 12 teaches that families may be torn apart, betraying one another. Then verse

---

7   B. M. F. van Iersel, "The Gospel According to St. Mark," *Nederlands Theologisch Tijd-schrift* 34 (January 1980): 20, 35.

8   The Greek phrase is emphatic due to its being placed first in the sentence and the repetition of the pronoun "yourself": *blepete de humeis eautous.*

13 makes the astonishing statement that the followers of Christ (starting with the inquisitive disciples) would be hated by everyone on account of Christ's name. Again, in verse 13, the promise of salvation is given to all those who persevere to the end (with perseverance taken here as a call to endure the suffering of persecution).

B. M. F. van Iersel has pointed out that reading Mark with persecution in view gives greater significance to the text, but he also finally admits, "This does not necessarily mean that there actually had to be persecutions at the very moment the book was written, divulged or read."[9] Van Iersel's investigation demonstrates that the persecution theme is prevalent in Mark. As he puts it, the meaning of the Gospel is "most pregnant" in a situation of persecution. However, the "pregnancy" of the text is best understood as the offspring of the relationship pictured between Christ and his followers. This relationship between Christ (the Son of God) and his followers produces a perpetual potential for persecution. The reader of the Gospel may or may not be in an actual situation of persecution, but the reader should understand that following the Christ of Mark carries with it the possibility of persecution and even martyrdom.

Persecution on Account of Christ

Our exploration of the arguments for thinking that Mark's original audience was suffering persecution has not proven that the Gospel's first readers were under attack for being Christian. What this exploration has shown, however, is that Jesus taught his disciples to expect persecution because of him. On this point, Matthew and Mark agree. As mentioned earlier, the second part of our exploration of Mark must explain in more detail why (according to Mark) the followers of Christ are so prone to facing persecution.

The key to unlocking the dynamic of persecution in Mark lies in understanding how his Gospel views discipleship. In 8:31, Christ speaks of his impending passion and the cross that is awaiting him. Then in 8:34, Christ states that any who wish to follow him must likewise be prepared to "take up his cross" and follow. Thus, the suffering of the disciples is in some manner

---

9   van Iersel, "The Gospel According to St. Mark," 35.

akin to the suffering of Christ. The way of Jesus is the way of the cross, and those who follow Jesus ought to expect also to travel the way of the cross.

Beyond chapter 8, more direct textual evidence exists that indicates a connection between Christ, discipleship, and persecution in Mark. The evidence of such a three-part relationship rests on two textual keys: (1) Mark's arrangement of the persecution passages in connection with the passion narratives and (2) the parallel usage of the phrase "for my sake." Three passages (8:34–9:1; 10:23–31; 13:9–13) share the phrase "for my sake." In 8:35, the one who loses his life "for my sake and the gospel's" will save it. In 10:29–30, the one who leaves family and houses "for my sake and for the gospel's sake" will receive a hundredfold reward in this age and eternal life beyond that. And in 13:9–13, Jesus instructs his followers to watch out because they will be arrested and will have to stand before governors and kings "for my sake" (v. 9) as a witness to the gospel. They are promised that they will be saved if they endure to the end. The phrase "for my sake" occurs only in these three instances in the Gospel of Mark.

Beyond just noticing the presence of the phrase, scholars have also pointed out that the placement of the phrase in Mark is significant. The phrase in Mark 8 follows the first passion prediction in Mark, and the phrase in Mark 10 is placed just before the third passion prediction. All occurrences of the phrase are sandwiched within the context of the passion story, thus linking the disciples with the suffering Jesus. When the disciples suffer on account of Christ in the Gospel of Mark, they suffer with the one who himself was nailed to a cross, which is part of the gospel story. Matthew speaks more in terms of the kingdom of heaven, while Mark talks about the gospel. But both accounts expect that the followers of Christ might suffer on account of their relation to him. Through the linking of the gospel and the suffering of the disciples for Christ's sake, discipleship and Christology appear integrally wed in the Gospel of Mark.

For Mark, the gospel mission holds together Jesus and his disciples. The gospel mission includes every aspect of both Jesus's life and death and the significant role he plays as the preacher of God's coming reign on the earth. This emphasis on gospel mission sort of begs for a cosmic showdown between eternal life and eternal death. The righteousness of God is unleashed in Mark's Gospel through the reigning Jesus, who demonstrates power and authority over the demons and over the grisly hearts of murderous men who would execute him unjustly on the cross. In one sense, then, all of Jesus's life and death in Mark's Gospel can be viewed in relation to 3:27 as a binding of the strong man, which Suzanne Henderson refers to as "the decisive subduing of the adversarial powers whose grip on the world is being loosened."[10] The gospel mission is a mission that involves nothing less than a reversal of power over the course of world events, a reversal of power symbolized in Mark's Gospel by the power of God ripping the temple veil at the very moment Jesus suffers his apparent defeat by death on the cross (15:38). Because the gospel mission concerns God's dominion, its certainty is secured. By the end of Mark's Gospel, the work of Jesus has been successful and approved by God so that the certainty of "God's coming rule has been . . . decisively secured."[11]

Keeping the gospel mission in view, Henderson further points out how the disciples are called not simply to Jesus but also to the gospel mission of which Jesus himself is such an integral part. The entire story of God and his dominion as prophesied through Isaiah is unfolding through Mark's picture of Jesus. When, in this story, Jesus calls the disciples to follow him, he calls them to follow him personally in the work he is accomplishing. Jesus tells his disciples, "Follow *me.*" Jesus calls his disciples to follow him in Mark 1:17, 2:14, and 8:34, with the first-person pronoun present each time, thus indicating that their call is not a generic following of a religion or a political action committee. Rather, the call is to follow Jesus himself.

The personal nature of this call is made clear by Peter, who says, "Behold, we have left everything and followed You" (10:28). The disciples left their families and jobs for this single purpose: to follow Jesus Christ. The Gospel of Mark is clear to point out that this following of Jesus means following also the kingship mission he is accomplishing. The Gospel of Mark unfolds the relationship between Christ and his followers as beginning with the call to be the presence of Christ but always accompanying that call with the expectation that the disciples will also join with Christ in announcing the coming of a new kingdom. The disciples are called to more than a profession of faith. They are called to join "the initiation of God's sovereign

---

10   Suzanne Watts Henderson, *Christology and Discipleship in the Gospel of Mark,* Society for New Testament Studies Monograph (Cambridge: Cambridge University Press, 2008), 17.

11   Henderson, *Christology and Discipleship,* 18.

action that brings salvation and is to end in a transformed universe."[12] They are called to faith, to *believe* (1:14–15). Being called for Christ's sake and for the sake of the gospel in Mark is similar to being called on account of righteousness in Matthew. Also in Mark 3:14, Jesus appoints twelve to be in his presence and to go out and preach, and, in this one verse, both of Henderson's controlling ideas are found: presence and practice. From the time of their calling, the disciples are called both to Christ's presence and to the practice of obedience.

From this concept of being called to the presence and practice of Christ, Henderson examines the six episodes of discipleship found in the Gospel of Mark.[13] She then argues that the story developed through these six episodes indicates that the disciples were instructed in participating in the gospel mission with Jesus from the beginning. However, the original disciples (like all disciples since) fail to grasp and embrace this missional participation so that, over time, a crisis develops between the calling of the disciples and their inability to live up to it. The disciples are censured in the Gospel for proving to be sluggish servants both of Christ and of the kingdom mission. By the end of Mark's Gospel, the disciples are found sleeping instead of keeping watch as Jesus commanded them at Gethsemane (14:37). In 14:49, all the disciples flee from Christ at his hour of need. And Peter — the same Peter who confessed, "You are the Christ," in 8:29 — by the end of chapter 14 actually denies three times that he even knows Jesus. The problem is not merely confessional; the disciples are pictured as being guilty of more than failing to realize the full scope of Jesus's messianic claims. The disciples refuse to act on the authority of the Christ who called them to his mission. When Jesus enlists the disciples, he enlists them as agents of his authority. When they slumber in the garden and fall to the schemes of earthly authorities, they cease to exercise the authority Christ himself had given them. Clearly, as was the case in Matthew, the faithfulness of the disciples is lacking, demonstrating that the promises of Christ are not secured by the disciples, but by Christ himself. The disciples are brought in to the

---

12   G. R. Beasley-Murray, "Matthew 6:33: The Kingdom of God and the Ethics of Jesus," in *Neues Testament und Ethik*, ed. Rudolf Schnackenburg (Freiburg: Herder, 1989), 88, referencing Mark 1:15.

13   The six episodes of discipleship interaction chronicled in Henderson's study are 1:16–20; 3:13–15; 4:1–34; 6:7–13; 6:30–44; and 6:45–52.

righteousness of Christ by calling, by grace. Mark's Gospel, like Matthew's, makes plain that the disciples will need a body broken and blood poured out for their salvation (14:22–25).

Synthesis: Persecution in Mark

Disciples are persecuted in Christ's place. In Mark, as in Matthew, the righteousness of Christ will perpetually (though not continuously) put the disciples in the way of persecution, just as Christ himself suffered persecution at the hands of the authorities. Christ is the Son of God who has come to announce his kingdom. He is the king who has demonstrated the power of God over the "strong man." Christ is the king who calls forth his followers and charges them to be heralds of the messianic kingdom. When this king is gone (a disappearance foretold in the three passion predictions) the disciples will be charged with proclaiming the kingship mission.[14] As they fulfill their charge, they will suffer for the sake of Christ and of the gospel of the kingdom — which is very similar to suffering, as Matthew says, for righteousness on account of Christ.

Disciples are missional and thus confrontational. Second, this connection between the disciples and Jesus is both personal and missional. Christ first calls the disciples to himself. Once he calls, he commissions them for his purposes. If the messianic king is truly king, he can be expected to give orders to his servants. If he orders them to speak,[15] he likewise authorizes them in their speech. If the authority with which Jesus spoke was offensive to the unbelieving public in his day, then the same authority may continue to cause the same offense when the disciples speak to unbelieving audiences of their own.

We find in the Gospel of Mark the same elements as those present in Matthew: Jesus is claiming and demonstrating kingship authority; the dis-

---

14 Even when he is gone, Christ has not abandoned the disciples, as Peter is told in 14:28 and 16:7. See also 13:11 for the context of persecution.

15 William C. Weinrich, *Spirit and Martyrdom: A Study of the Work of the Holy Spirit in Contexts of Persecution and Martyrdom in the New Testament and Early Christian Literature* (Washington, DC: University Press of America, 1981), 17–22, argues for the spiritual necessity of proclamation and persecution.

ciples display his righteousness through their service (faith/obedience); and those who show this allegiance to Christ may expect persecution, even as Christ himself suffered persecution to the point of death on a cross. The Gospel of Mark does not contradict Matthew. As Colbert pointed out to the skeptic on his show, Matthew and Mark use their own language to describe the same Jesus from different perspectives. So Mark does not use the word "righteousness" much, and he only mentions the adjective "righteous" on two occasions. Nevertheless, Mark presents the same picture of Jesus as that portrayed in Matthew: he is the Son of God (Mark 1:1, 11); he has authority over the kingdom of God (1:15); he has authority over his disciples (1:16–20); he holds authority over the Sabbath law (2:23–28); and he alone has authority to forgive sins (2:1–12). When the disciples act by faith in obedience to their sovereign king, they are personally connected both to their Lord and to his mission.

Disciples suffer for Christ's sake. Finally, Christ identifies the persecution in relation to himself. He is the root cause. Just as in Matthew, so too in Mark, persecution happens because of Christ ("for my sake"). Christ is personally impacted by and somehow present in the episodes of persecution. Indeed, the gospel and the kingdom in Mark are related to the Christ, who suffered on the cross. But this gospel is also related to Christ the sovereign Lord who will separate humankind at the final judgment (13:24–27). The tension, introduced at the first coming of Christ, will not subside until his final return. In the meantime, those aligned with him and his mission will find themselves misaligned with the world and its mission.

Matthew (kingdom, righteousness) and Mark (gospel, discipleship) use different language, but they both consistently portray Jesus as the central figure in Christian persecution. They also both expect persecution to arise perpetually against Christ's disciples on account of their Lord and his mission.

6

LUKE-ACTS: PERSECUTION IN
SALVATION HISTORY AND THE EARLY CHURCH

*Through many tribulations we must enter the kingdom
of God.*

(Acts 14:22)

Pastors wake up with hopeful expectations most Sunday mornings. Often, however, Sundays supply the unexpected. Even if Pastor Ezekiel Omidiji were expecting the unexpected, he couldn't have been prepared for what happened on a Sunday morning in July just before the start of the worship service of the ECWA Gospel 1 Church in Jos, Nigeria.

Around 8:45, Pastor Ezekiel and his congregation were rocked by an explosion in a nearby field. As it turned out, the explosion was a bomb that only minutes before had been ticking on the restroom floor of the church facility. A security man entered the restroom and heard the mechanical ticking. Like a scene from a James Bond thriller, the drama was intense. The man picked up the bomb and ran with it to a nearby field, throwing it over the fence just before it blew up. That was the explosion that startled the pastor and his congregants. And this bomb was not alone. Officials called to the scene found a second bomb, which was also active. Officials detonated it, keeping the congregation safe from whoever had intended them harm.

What the congregation did next might surprise you. Imagine a church setting in America where two active bombs had just been found and detonated. Fire trucks, squad cars, helicopters, and SWAT vans would busily control the parking lot. Crime scene tape would surround the facility and grounds. And police barricades would seal off the streets to both pedestrian and vehicular traffic. Everyone would give thanks to God and most likely go home to hug their families.

In Jos, Nigeria, Christians cannot afford to live under the illusion of safety. They live as many of the first Christians did, knowing that "through many tribulations we must enter the kingdom of God" (Acts 14:22). This church had been targeted and threatened in the past. They knew of stories from other places in Nigeria where worshipers would flee from bombs in buildings only to be gunned down by Islamic militants as they tried to run away. The Christians in Jos simply completed the task they had originally intended for this Sunday morning in July. They worshiped the Lord Jesus Christ together.

Such perseverance is not unknown in the history of Christianity. It has often been the norm. In Acts 14, for instance, Paul and Barnabas both bask in the sunshine of a spiritual revival at Iconium and later flee for their lives from the place. They run away from Iconium to Lystra, where they are worshiped as gods, only to be persecuted again. Paul is actually stoned there and left to die. The journey for a Christian from the ecstasies of spiritual awakenings to the agonies of murderous assaults is neither long nor far. It can happen quickly. The persecution of the church at Jos is very much in concert with the history of Christians suffering in the name of Christ. As Paul and Barnabas summarize the matter in Acts 14:22, rest in the kingdom of God is no easy matter. The kingdom way is often the way of persecution.

As we have done with Matthew and Mark, we now attempt to do with Luke and Acts: explore why the New Testament links persecution so closely with Christ and his followers. Fortunately, one scholar has produced a substantial book that examines persecution in the books of Luke and Acts. Sounding similar to the conclusions we have reached from the Old Testament, Matthew, and Mark, Scott Cunningham summarizes his study this way: "The narrative [of Luke-Acts] shows an awareness that persecution may come from Gentiles as well as Jews. Where Christ is proclaimed, the status quo is upset and there will be people, both Jews and Gentiles, who will resist this change. Jesus is not only the cause of division in Israel; he also produces division among the Gentiles (Luke 12: 51–53)."[1]

---

1   Scott Cunningham, *"Through Many Tribulations": The Theology of Persecution in Luke-Acts,* JSNTSup 142 (Sheffield: Sheffield Academic, 1997), 307.

Cunningham's book takes its main title from Acts 14:22: *"Through Many Tribulations."* Cunningham's work focuses on persecution as opposed to martyrdom. Though Cunningham recognizes how important it is for all Christians to understand persecution, he is most concerned to help Christians like those in Jos, Nigeria. Cunningham chose to study Luke and Acts in part because of the prevalence of the persecution theme throughout the two books. According to Cunningham, all but six chapters in Luke-Acts contain instruction concerning persecution. Of these six chapters, five are in the Gospel; only one chapter in Acts fails to mention persecution (chapter 27, which chronicles Paul's shipwreck on his perilous journey to Rome). The prevalence of persecution throughout Luke and Acts leads Cunningham to suspect that Luke's audience was likely suffering persecution, although he admits that such prevalence does not necessarily "imply anything about whether or not persecution is part of [the reader's] current situation."[2] In the previous chapter (on Mark), we considered in detail the kinds of arguments put forward for placing readers in a situation of persecution, so we can forgo such a discussion related to Luke and Acts.

Six Theological Functions of Persecution in Luke-Acts

Cunningham examines Luke and Acts as a single literary narrative. He believes the same author of Luke's Gospel also wrote the book of Acts as a follow-up to and fuller development of the ongoing spread of Jesus's gospel mission through the early church (see Luke 1:1–4 and Acts 1:1). Cunningham's foremost concern is the overall content of the narrative, not its potential reaction. He argues that Luke-Acts consistently links the followers of Jesus to Christ himself in order to demonstrate the ongoing nature of salvation history. Cunningham means by this close identification of Christ with his followers that the two books serve as a history of God with his people. For Cunningham, such a history can be observed through the persecution of his people. With persecution in mind, the reader of Luke-Acts may be tempted to ask the practical and theological question as to whether he too might suffer on account of Christ like the believers in Acts. As further comment on that question, Cunningham offers six theological functions of persecution in Acts.

---

2 Cunningham, *"Through Many Tribulations,"* 329.

First, the persecution portrait in the book of Acts displays the reality of God's providence. Persecution is part of the plan of God. To Cunningham, persecution is never pictured as an "accident" or "surprise." Rather, persecution is an aspect of divine providence. In Cunningham's view, episodes of persecution act to fulfill the prophecies of Jesus recorded in the Gospel of Luke (21:12; 24:44–49). Jesus acts as a prophet of God, revealing the will of God to the people of God who follow him. Persecution (as Jesus predicted) verifies that Jesus is true in all he says about the future of his people.

Second, persecution is pictured in Luke-Acts as the rejection of God's agents by those who are supposedly God's people. Here, Cunningham's thesis undergoes an undulation of sorts as he considers the conflict Christians experience in both Jewish and Gentile contexts. For him, the central focus of the persecution in Luke-Acts "is clearly on the rejection of the salvation of God and the persecution of the agents of God *by Israel*, those who are supposedly the people of God."[3] The Christian church grew out of the soil of Jewish faith. Admitting that *most* of the early conflict occurred with the Jews, then, is as natural as a botanist recognizing that most of a tree's early life depends on the interaction it has with the soil. The botanist would also realize, however, that later threats such as lightning, wind, rain, and insects would affect the tree too.

Without addressing questions about whether Acts offers reliable history, Cunningham opts instead to explain persecution in terms of Luke's theological agenda, emphasizing the conflict between Jews and Christians. While it is true that much of the persecution in Luke-Acts is instigated by Jews, Cunningham may overstate the case by *defining* persecution in Luke-Acts as the rejection of God's salvation *by Israel*. Even if Luke-Acts emphasizes the real conflict between Jews and Christians, still that does not mean that persecution — in its essence — originates from the Jews. Perhaps more important, the issue with persecution is the rejection of God's salvation — regardless of whether that rejection is from Jews or Gentiles. Ultimately, this appears to be the crux of the persecution matter in Luke and Acts.

Third, Cunningham argues that the persecuted people of God stand in continuity with God's prophets. Because Cunningham and other New Testament scholars make so much of identifying with the prophets, I will spend

---

3   Cunningham, "*Through Many Tribulations*," 302; emphasis original.

more energy exploring this third theological function than I do for the other five functions. Cunningham appeals to the connection with the prophets on display in the sermon of Stephen to make this point. Stephen tells his audience that they are in league with those of Israel's past who always resist the Holy Spirit and, instead of listening to the prophets, kill them (Acts 7:51–52). Because Stephen is killed just after this pronouncement, he is counted by Cunningham as being in line with the very prophets who were killed by past generations of stiff-necked rebels.

Though it is not unwarranted to draw such conclusions, it is also not necessary to do so in a strictly literal sense. Simply because Stephen was killed for preaching a sermon in which the audience was implicated in killing the prophets does not mean that Stephen himself was considered a prophet. In what sense is the relation between Stephen and the prophets secured? Might it not be possible for Stephen to be related to the prophets in his preaching of righteousness, yet not necessarily be deemed one of the prophets? Why not, rather, assume that Stephen is an apostle since Jesus is recorded earlier in the Luke-Acts corpus as foretelling the persecution of prophets and apostles (Luke 11:49)? The point is to say that the link between the prophets and Stephen may be the same link we noticed from Matthew: both the prophets and Stephen were in the line of Christ's righteousness in the face of stiff-necked rebellion against God.

In other sections of his book, Cunningham repeats the claim that Christians suffering persecution are linked directly to the Old Testament prophets. Once again, however, the case concerning prophet identification is not as strong as it first appears. Cunningham says, "The disciples are sure to suffer persecution, because that is what happened to God's prophets before them."[4] Surprisingly, the text to which Cunningham is referring nowhere asserts such a causal relation between the persecution of the disciples and the persecution of the prophets. Rather, the text (Luke 6:23) asserts that the followers of Jesus are blessed and ought to rejoice in their persecutions because the same people who are persecuting the followers of Christ once also persecuted the prophets (vicariously through their forefathers). The idea, then, is that the disciples can be encouraged because they are proving to be *true* followers of God on account of who their enemies are. They are

---

4   Cunningham, *"Through Many Tribulations,"* 72–73.

not being taught that their persecution happens because they are prophets or because that is the fate of prophets before them. In fact, Luke 6:22 states unequivocally that the root of persecution is "for the sake of the Son of Man."

The reflex of establishing continuity between Christians and the prophets is ultimately inadequate as a framework for understanding the persecution dynamic in Luke-Acts. Asserting a relationship back to the prophets only begs the question, "Why were the prophets persecuted?" A simple statement from Cunningham illustrates the inadequacy of the concept of prophet for explaining persecution. He writes, "The disciples are sure to experience persecution because that was the fate of the true prophets before them."[5] The persecution is not *because* of the prophets. Cunningham adds a necessary qualifier to the term "prophet," indicating that the persecution does not occur because of an identity as prophet. Rather, the persecution occurs because of the identity as *true* — true proclaimers of the righteousness of God, like the persecuted prophets of old.

The simplicity of this analysis needs no explanation beyond the example of the prophet Micaiah, who appeared to stand alone against Ahab as a proclaimer of the truth (1 Kings 22). Micaiah alone preached the righteousness of God, even though Ahab is reported to have had about four hundred prophets in his service. There were many prophets in Israel who were never persecuted. The prophets who were persecuted were thus mistreated not simply because they were prophets but because they were, as Cunningham says, "true." And they were true prophets in the face of opposition to God.

What I am saying is that the significance of true extends backward all the way to Abel, whose blood was the first righteous blood spilled, and forward to its fulfillment in Christ, whose blood was ultimately the divinely acceptable righteous blood spilled (Luke 11:49–51). So the supplemental modifier "true" carries more significant force than the title "prophet." Jesus taught in Luke that his followers would continue to suffer persecution in the same way the righteous prophets always suffered on account of God.

For Luke, just as for Matthew, the prophets were not the ultimate issue because "something greater than Jonah is here" (Luke 11:32). The issue of offense is not prophecy per se, but a true proclamation of righteousness. With this clarification in view, we can agree with Cunningham's conclusion that

---

5 Cunningham, "*Through Many Tribulations*," 310.

"the persecution of Jesus and his disciples are [sic] clearly presented by the narrative in terms of a continuation of the pattern of the rejection of God's messengers typical of Israel's salvation-history."[6] True messengers like true prophets will face persecution — not because they are prophets, but because they are truly representing the righteousness of God in Christ.

Fourth, Cunningham concludes that persecution functions theologically in Luke-Acts to demonstrate that following Jesus is all it takes to make one a target of persecution. In other words, persecution is a clear consequence of belonging to Jesus Christ. Cunningham's assertion here is affirmation of what we have been observing thus far from Genesis through Mark. Cunningham asserts that Jesus himself serves as the root provocateur of persecution. All of the particular components of this theological function will be examined in more detail below as we continue to explore how persecution is related to Christ, righteousness, and the kingdom of God.

The fifth function of persecution in Luke-Acts is to display Christian perseverance. Persecution acts as an occasion through which the Christian demonstrates perseverance in the faith. Cunningham views the need for the saints to persevere in the face of persecution as a primary encouragement of the persecution theme in Luke-Acts.

A great example of persecution leading to perseverance is found in the narrative of Paul in Corinth (Acts 18). Frustrated, Paul shook out his garments and intended to leave the city because of its belligerent refusal to hear the truth. Instead of leaving town, however, Paul stopped at the home of Titius Justus. Then Crispus — the leader of the synagogue — was suddenly converted. And Paul was told by God to stop being afraid, "but go on speaking and do not be silent; for I am with you, and no man will attack you in order to harm you, for I have many people in this city" (18:9–10). In a hurry to leave on account of opposition to the gospel, Paul ended up staying for a year and a half, preaching the gospel and seeing the work of the kingdom increase. Persecution led to perseverance.

Finally, the sixth theological function of persecution in Luke-Acts is to demonstrate the reality of divine triumph. As Cunningham puts it, "Persecution cannot stop the growth of the Word of God."[7] Building his case (as

---

6 Cunningham, *"Through Many Tribulations,"* 311.

7 Cunningham, *"Through Many Tribulations,"* 321.

others have done)[8] from the intervention of Gamaliel in Acts 5, Cunningham concludes, "The message of salvation in Jesus *is* of God, and therefore, as the narrative of Acts in particular demonstrates, the persecutors are unable to halt the growth [of] the movement."[9] Cunningham demonstrates that the Word of God grows both *in spite of* and *because of* persecution. The persecution that begins as a potential defeater for the followers of Christ ends with a victory through God's sovereign power.

By offering these six theological functions, Cunningham hopes to avoid oversimplifying the vast array of instructions found in Luke's two volumes. For Cunningham, the picture of persecution in Luke-Acts cannot be condensed into a single framework. One can find, however, woven in and through the six functions Cunningham enumerates, the single thread of Christ establishing the kingdom of God displaying the righteousness of God.

Four Further Characteristics of Persecution in Luke-Acts

Moving the discussion forward, Cunningham next identifies four significant characteristics of the persecution episodes in Luke and Acts. He calls these characteristics corollaries. The corollaries are further descriptions of how persecution functions in Luke and Acts. Three of these four corollaries focus closer attention on Christ. The fourth corollary focuses attention on Christ's kingdom mission.

The first corollary is the foundation of *prophecy*. Christ acts as prophet in Luke's Gospel, and the prophecies he makes are fulfilled in Acts. For example, in Luke 12:11–12 and 21:12–19, Jesus warns his followers that they will be thrust out of the synagogues and put on trial before kings and governors and rulers for his sake and for the gospel. The book of Acts then chronicles Peter, Paul, and the other disciples being tossed out of the synagogues and ultimately having to go before rulers — with Paul finally appealing to go before Caesar in Rome. Clearly, Jesus prophesies faithfully. However, we should remember that Luke has in mind a greater claim for Jesus than merely

---

8   Brian Rapske, "Opposition to the Plan of God and Persecution," in *Witness to the Gospel: The Theology of Acts*, ed. I. Howard Marshall and David Peterson (Grand Rapids: Eerdmans, 1998), 235–56.

9   Cunningham, *"Through Many Tribulations,"* 322.

prophet. Recall Luke 11:32: "The men of Nineveh will rise up at the judgment with this generation and condemn it, for they repented at the preaching of Jonah, and behold, something greater than Jonah is here."

Luke says in the beginning of the Gospel that he is writing out in orderly fashion all the things that took place in the ministry of Jesus (1:3). The orderly account Luke offers pushes the reader to recognize a great crescendo of victory at Christ's being raised from the dead. Christ is indeed a prophet of the kingdom of God after John the Baptist (16:16). Yet the status of Christ is unique, as Luke's comparison with John makes plain. John was called "the prophet of the Most High" (1:76), but Christ was called "Son of the Most High" (1:32) and "Son of God" (1:35) and was promised that he would reign on the throne of David forever (1:32–33).

The two books of Luke and Acts make much of the notion of Christ's authority, especially in relation to persecution. After noticing the declaration in Luke 11:32 that something greater than Jonah is here, the reader begins to see more clearly that Jesus is no mere prophet. From the early chapters, Jesus was demonstrated to be the Son of God (chapter 3) who preached the kingdom of God (4:43). By the end of the Gospel, the unfolding drama makes all too plain the identity and divine authority — the regnal righteousness — of this man who had to face the world's execution.

Not coincidentally, before he dies, Jesus instructs his followers (Luke 21:12–19) in the reality of the persecution they will face. First, Jesus tells his followers that their persecution is "for my name's sake."[10] Their persecution is not linked to prophetic identification as much as it is to identification with Jesus, who, in the passage, is pictured as the one for whose sake they would stand to be judged by kings and governors (21:12). This is the dynamic we have called regnal righteousness. The offense leading to persecution originates with the righteousness of God in Jesus Christ.

Cunningham's second persecution corollary is that persecution will lead to *witness*. In other words, the witness of Jesus's followers, spoken of in Luke 21:12–13, is itself the consequence of their persecution: "They will lay their hands on you and persecute you, delivering you up to the synagogues and

---

10 This phrase in Luke is synonymous with Matthew's "on account of me." Luke uses the more common Greek preposition *dia* rather than the irregular preposition *'eneken* as was prevalent in Matthew's Gospel, but the idea is surely the same: the name (authority) of the kingly Christ is enough to get the disciples persecuted.

prisons, and you will be brought before kings and governors for my name's sake. This will be your opportunity to bear witness" (ESV). The consequential nature of this witness is displayed in the language and construction of the verse. Verse 13 clearly means "to turn out, lead to."[11] The persecution in verse 12 leads to the witness opportunity in verse 13. Thus witnessing is a consequence of persecution, not a cause. The cause is Christ (reigning, ruling in righteousness). He is the voice behind the preaching of his followers. So improving Cunningham's first corollary, we might say that Christ's followers do suffer *in fulfillment of* Christ's prophecy, but more important, they suffer persecution as they do *because* of Christ himself. And their suffering will lead to their witnessing for him.

According to the second corollary, the disciples are persecuted *like* Jesus, meaning in the same manner as Jesus. While Cunningham often links persecution back to the suffering of the prophets, he also maintains a unique place for Christ. Christ (not the prophet) is the primary guide for explaining persecution.

Cunningham makes another helpful distinction when he notes that Luke's view of persecution is not one in which the disciples *imitate* Christ; rather, persecution is the *continuation* of what began in Christ. Some scholars have sought to define persecution as an imitation of Jesus, but imitation is an inadequate foundation. The reason imitation is inadequate is that it assumes persecution is rooted in Christ's followers — in what they do in order to suffer as Jesus suffered. Anchoring theological and ethical definitions in the motives of Christ's followers is dubious. Consider how fine the line between doing what is right and doing what is right in order to be made much of (like the Pharisees). Luke and the other New Testament writers don't anchor persecution in the motives or actions of Christ's followers. Instead, the New Testament grounds persecution in who Christ is. The disciples do not so much imitate Christ as they continue serving his mission, thereby continuing the opportunity for the rejection of his work. Their mission is his mission, and they will suffer (as he did) seeking to accomplish it.

In his third corollary, Cunningham reinforces the point that persecution of the followers of Christ happens because of their association with

---

11   I. Howard Marshall, *The Gospel of Luke: A Commentary on the Greek Text,* New International Greek Testament Commentary (Grand Rapids: Eerdmans, 1978), 767.

Jesus. Disciples are not persecuted on account of their personal holiness or their own righteousness; rather, they are persecuted because of their allegiance to Jesus Christ. In this persecution, the disciples are identified with Jesus, and Jesus is identified with them. Cunningham insists that in identification with Jesus one finds that "the disciple's persecution is given its firmest foundation."[12]

Strangely, Cunningham does not make explicit the nature of this firm foundation. Quoting from the conversion of Saul, in which Jesus asks, "Saul, Saul, why are you persecuting me?" Cunningham concludes that Luke does not define the nature of the identification between the disciples and the Lord. In discussing this third corollary, Cunningham leaves the nature of identification unstated, while in other places, he tends to attribute the nature of the identification to be prophetic continuation (as noted above). Yet the righteousness of God in Jesus Christ explains better the nature of the relationship between Christ and his followers. Christ brings his followers into fellowship with God in the already unfolding kingdom of heaven. Consider how neatly Luke 21:12–19 summarizes several of the persecution themes we have studied thus far:

> But before all these things, they will lay their hands on you and will persecute you, delivering you to the synagogues and prisons, bringing you before kings and governors for My name's sake. It will lead to an opportunity for your testimony. So make up your minds not to prepare beforehand to defend yourselves; for I will give you utterance and wisdom which none of your opponents will be able to resist or refute. But you will be betrayed even by parents and brothers and relatives and friends, and they will put some of you to death, and you will be hated by all because of My name. Yet not a hair of your head will perish. By your endurance you will gain your lives.

The hatred that fuels persecution is against the name of Jesus (21:17). The conversion account of Saul of Tarsus demonstrates that persecution of followers of Christ is persecution of Christ himself (Acts 9:4–5). And Jesus promises that he will remain present with his people in their witness through

---

12   Cunningham, *"Through Many Tribulations,"* 318.

persecution (Luke 21:15). Though Luke uses different language and offers a different perspective, still his view of persecution in Luke-Acts displays the regnal righteousness dynamic as clearly as does Matthew. The regnal dynamic agrees with Cunningham that alignment with Jesus is the firmest foundation for understanding the persecution of Christ's followers.

The final corollary is not related specifically to Christ. Instead, the fourth corollary is missiological, meaning that it is related to God's ongoing mission in the world. In this fourth corollary, Cunningham explores more closely the function of *witness*. Persecution is an unsurprising consequence of the disciples' lives as they faithfully obey God's command to witness to the ends of the earth.

This idea of witnessing in relation to persecution is personified in the life of Paul. Perhaps significantly, Paul is not pictured in Acts as a prophet; rather, he is an apostle, even though he is often found in the company of prophets. From the beginning of his ministry (Acts 9:15–16), Paul learns that he must suffer for the name of Christ as he bears this name among the Gentiles. Such name-bearing is categorized as missiological because it seeks to extend the works of Christ to the remotest places of the earth. The name-bearing is evangelistic. Yet bearing the name of Christ is more than evangelistic, too, as it means being called "Christian," the way disciples in Antioch were first called by that highest of names (11:26). *Christian* represents being identified with Christ and living in the promises that he offers his people. Name-bearing means representing as well as proclaiming Christ. One could say that the missiological task unfolds the witness to the righteousness of God to all nations (1:6–8). This name-bearing and proclaiming calls attention to Christ — and thereby generates persecution on account of him. When the disciples are persecuted on account of him, they offer witness in response.

From these corollaries, Cunningham draws this firm conclusion: "For Luke then persecution is an integral part of what it means to be a follower of Jesus. To be identified with him and to witness about him means to invite persecution."[13]

With the clarifications noted throughout this chapter, Cunningham's six theological functions and four corollaries affirm the points we have observed thus far from Genesis through Mark. The functions (revised from our study) can be summarized as follows:

---

13 Cunningham, *"Through Many Tribulations,"* 319.

- Persecution is part of God's plan.
- Persecution is pictured in Luke-Acts as the rejection of God's agents.
- The persecuted stand in a long line of the righteous, which includes the Old Testament prophets.
- Persecution is instigated simply by identifying with Jesus.
- Persecution functions to display perseverance in faith.
- Persecution demonstrates the reality of God's triumph.

The four corollaries might be summarized in this manner:

- Persecution in Acts fulfills the prophecies Christ made in Luke.
- Persecution leads to opportunities for witnessing.
- Persecution happens on account of being identified with Jesus.
- Persecution accomplishes God's mission over time.

Through the books of Luke and Acts, one can learn much about what persecution is and why it happens. All in all, Cunningham affirms what we have learned thus far. Persecution happens now as it always has — on account of Christ. Pastor Ezekiel Omidiji and his congregation in Jos, Nigeria, understand what Luke means: being a faithful witness of Christ's salvation is to invite persecution. To put it another way, the early church believed that Christians must go through many tribulations to enter the kingdom of God. Pastor Ezekiel would have no trouble affirming this notion. In the following chapter, we will explore whether the apostle Paul would agree.

7

PAUL'S LETTERS: PERSECUTION AND
THE RIGHTEOUSNESS OF CHRIST

> *Now I rejoice in my sufferings for your sake, and in my*
> *flesh I am filling up what is lacking in Christ's afflictions*
> *for the sake of his body, that is, the church.*
> *(Col. 1:24 ESV)*

A young woman named Akua lives as a fugitive. She is not a criminal, but to her family she is beyond reach.

After becoming a Christian, the teenager had to flee from her Muslim family for her own safety. Akua lives in the West African nation of Ghana — a nation that not long ago was 60 percent Christian, but now is majority Muslim. When Akua accepted Christ, her family rejected her. In a desperate attempt to keep her in the Muslim faith, her family gave her in marriage to a 40-year-old Muslim cleric, who already had two wives. Akua, desiring neither to be Muslim nor married to this man, ran away to a secret location where she lives as discretely as possible among her Christian brothers and sisters. Such are the perils these days of living as a Christian in Ghana.

With firsthand knowledge of the persecution and oppression prevalent in his home country of Ghana, J. S. Pobee devoted his Cambridge studies to understanding persecution and martyrdom. The result of this study is his published work on the subject: *Persecution and Martyrdom in the Theology of*

Paul.[1] As the title indicates, this work focuses on Paul's writings, attempting to develop the themes of persecution and martyrdom from their historical roots. If Pobee is correct, then Paul's writings expose *zeal* as the root provocateur of Christian persecution, which is to say, persecution is a sure sign of being zealous for the Lord. In Pobee's own words, "Persecution occurs as a manifestation of conflicting zeals."[2]

To consider this thesis in more detail, we begin with the forms of persecution found in Paul's writings. Paul mentions the arena, crucifixion, the sword, stoning, burning, imprisonment, expulsion, and corporal punishment (see 2 Cor. 11:22–28). From his review of these forms, Pobee draws two conclusions: (1) that the Romans maintained the right of the sword of justice, thus taking responsibility for enforcing punishments, particularly for enforcing capital punishment; and (2) that, as a result, the New Testament depiction of the Jews is to be considered "a tendentious statement which needs to be taken *cum grano salis.*"[3] One may rightly wonder how it is that a survey of the forms of persecution found in the writings of Paul ends with a statement that discredits those writings. What does Pobee mean that we should take Paul's portrait of the Jews "with a grain of salt"?

We should pause at this point to consider Pobee's approach to the New Testament because his treatment of Paul's writings will be affected by what he considers those passages to be. Does he believe Paul's writings are reliable accounts of historical events? Do Paul's writings offer authoritative instruction? Or does Pobee think Paul's letters are mythical accounts from a superstitious people? Are they culturally conditioned political responses?

Pobee treats the writings of Paul and the New Testament with great respect. This respect is evident in the attention he gives to the original Greek in formulating his argument that persecution demonstrates the presence of zealous faith. Nevertheless, in establishing his formulation of Paul's persecution dynamic, Pobee leans heavily (possibly too heavily) on sources outside the Bible. Because of the higher value he gives to these extra-biblical sources, Pobee thinks it is appropriate to take the New Testament accounts of Judaism

---

1   J. S. Pobee, *Persecution and Martyrdom in the Theology of Paul*, JSNTSup 6 (Sheffield: JSOT, 1985).

2   Pobee, *Persecution and Martyrdom*, 118.

3   Pobee, *Persecution and Martyrdom*, 12. The Latin phrase means "with a grain of salt."

"with a grain of salt," as though the New Testament were the product of a small group of Jews with a theological axe to grind.

The truth, of course, may be that the early Christians — like the Maccabeans and the Romans — had a kind of axe to grind, but they are not by that fact discredited or to be diminished in what they are saying, particularly (as Gamaliel points out in Acts 5) if the axe they are grinding were itself in step with the Spirit of God. Or, to make the point differently, the early Christian writers had both a particular perspective and an expressed agenda, just as all writers always do. Christians knowingly give preference to the writings of the apostles.

Pobee's approach to the New Testament is clearly historical-critical. He believes theology emerges from the experience of a people. He probably means by this that theology does not evolve but, rather, comes about because of personal experiences shared in a community of faith. This would, of course, be true in a manner reminiscent of how Paul's theology emerged from his experience on the Damascus Road.

However, more needs to be said. Is it experience alone that generates theology? Is there (or can there be) a theology behind and responsible for the experience? Is God capable of forming and shaping a community by his Word? The point is, Pobee assumes that the community decides the shape of theology, rather than assuming that theology fundamentally determines the shape of the community. As a result, the greater portion of *Persecution and Martyrdom* explores the context of the community that he assumes formed Christianity. He believes the Judaism of the Maccabees primarily shaped Christian thinking about persecution. The Maccabees era took place about two centuries before Christ and clearly had an impact on the thinking of Jews in the first century.

Out of this Maccabees framework, Pobee asserts that the Maccabean martyrs formed the early Christian perspective on persecution. The Maccabees were heroes in Jewish history on account of their rebellion against the Seleucid dynasty in the second century BC. Jews today still celebrate Hanukkah, which is a festival marking the rededication of the temple in Jerusalem after the victory of the Maccabees. Those who died in the struggle for Jewish independence are revered in Jewish history as the Maccabean martyrs. The Maccabeans prized the idea of a suffering hero. In this framework, the martyr is one who is zealous to obey the Lord and, because of that zeal, ends up suffering at the hands of godless men (as in the death of Judah Maccabee). The early Christians then presumably linked Jesus with these earlier Jewish martyrs.

For Pobee, this link between Jesus and the Jewish martyrs would provide a solution to the scandal of the cross. Pobee believes Christians adopted this framework to explain how the cross might become "good news." In other words, a Jew from the first century would have had serious problems with the idea of a crucified messiah. He would have been unable to accept such a concept because Scripture says that anyone who hangs on a tree is cursed (Deut. 21:23). Those Jews, then, who were followers of Christ would need to make sense out of seeing their leader hanging as a cursed man on a tree. So (as Pobee's theory goes) their experience was interpreted through the first-century lens of martyrdom provided by the Maccabean community. In this Maccabean framework, leaders who were zealous for obedience were, in a sense, "asking for it." Their zeal caused them to be a target for persecution. In Paul's writings, then, Jesus became the new prototype of the Jewish martyr.

In developing this Maccabean martyr framework, Pobee relies primarily on Maccabean sources, rather than building his case on biblical sources. He has constructed an historical context behind the biblical text and then used that context to interpret the text. His confidence in this historical construction enables him to take the information from the Scriptures with a grain of salt. This approach leaves Pobee somewhat detached from Old Testament literature, which obviously influenced the first Christians. Pobee also does not engage with important passages from the New Testament.

To be sure, Pobee does not completely ignore the Old Testament. He interacts, for instance, with the book of Daniel. Yet, his interaction with Daniel is roughly equivalent to his study of 1 Maccabees, and his interaction with the Old Testament as a whole is less than his study of non-biblical literature. The New Testament writers, on the other hand, are far more concerned with the Old Testament than they are with these extra-biblical writings. Pobee does not reflect that dynamic in his development of the themes of persecution and martyrdom. As a result, he does not make full use of the Scriptures in his explanation. Two brief examples illustrate this point.

First, Pobee sees a clear connection between Jesus's death and the martyrdom of the seven sons and their mother recorded in 4 Maccabees 16–17. However, he refuses to acknowledge any relationship between Paul's portrait of a crucified Messiah and the picture of the Suffering Servant in Isaiah 53. Other scholars readily accept the validity of considering 4 Maccabees without excluding Isaiah 53. Most scholars, in fact, see a reflection of Isaiah's Suffering Servant in Paul's portrait of persecution.

Biblical scholars have long noted a connection between the humiliation of Christ leading to his exaltation in Philippians 2 and the way Isaiah portrays a humiliated servant leading God's people to salvation in Isaiah 53. According to Pobee, those scholars have misread the Isaiah text. Pobee argues that the Isaiah passage does not say that the exaltation of the servant is the result of the humiliation. He believes the connection between humiliation and glorification is an afterthought (a kind of "add-on") from the early church to help make sense of Christ dying on the cross. The text of Isaiah, however, betrays Pobee's rejection of this passage. As one scholar points out concerning Isaiah 53, "The language there suggests that the exaltation is some kind of resurrection, but whatever its precise meaning, the exaltation is clearly a *consequence of and reward for the humiliation and death*."[4] Isaiah 53:12, for instance, twice confirms a consequential relationship, using both "therefore" and "because": "Therefore, I will allot Him a portion with the great, and He will divide the booty with the strong; because He poured out Himself to death, and was numbered with the transgressors; yet He Himself bore the sin of many, and interceded for the transgressors."

As a result of his decision not to allow influence from Isaiah 53, Pobee is unable to draw out completely the picture Paul actually paints in Philippians, a picture that has direct implications for Christians suffering persecution. Paul exhorts Christians in Philippians 2 to have the humiliation-to-exaltation mindset of their Lord, and throughout the epistle Paul urges these believers to work out their salvation, to stand firm in Christ through trials even unto death. In living this way — with the mindset of Christ (and Paul) — the Philippian Christians could expect both that God would supply their needs and that their faith would show the futility of those who oppose them (1:28). In other words, like the Suffering Servant, these Philippian Christians would see their humiliation turn to exaltation. Ultimately, the mindset called for in Philippians 2 is a mindset given to the righteousness of Christ, who sacrificed

---

4 Michael Gorman, *Cruciformity: Paul's Narrative Spirituality of the Cross* (Grand Rapids: Eerdmans, 2001), 317; emphasis original.

himself for others so that they might become partakers of the kingdom (see 2 Cor. 5:21). This humiliation to exaltation of God's Messiah was certainly foreshadowed by Isaiah.

A second way to see how Pobee shortchanges important biblical passages is in his overlooking instructions from Jesus about persecution. So, for example, Pobee does not mention Matthew 5:10–12, a passage that we've noticed is significant for understanding persecution. In that passage, Jesus more than hints at the reality of persecution befalling his followers. In his description, Jesus includes slander and lying as persecution when they occur against his followers on account of his name. Pobee fails to consider the rich implications of such instruction from Christ and how Paul might have been influenced by it.

Paul instructs the Christians in Rome to suffer slander and reproach on behalf of Christ, using Christ as the example. Quoting the Old Testament, Paul writes of Christ in Romans 15:3, "The reproaches of those who reproached you fell on me," thus demonstrating the nature of Christ's suffering on behalf of others. Paul, in turn, encouraged the Christians of Rome to suffer reproach, so that through endurance and through the encouragement of the Scriptures they might have hope.

Paul himself had suffered much slander and false accusations. He had endured reproach for the cause of Christ, as the book of Acts is quick and thorough to report. Persecution was stirred up against Paul and Barnabas in Antioch because of the slanderous remarks some of the Jews made to the leading women in the region (13:13–51, esp. vv. 50–51). Likewise, in Lystra, false accusations were made against Paul, and, as a result, he was stoned and left for dead. He was falsely accused and imprisoned. Then, he was falsely charged with capital offenses that landed him before governors and kings (14:8–20, esp. vv. 19–20). As was noted earlier, many interpreters believe the trials in Acts are a kind of "fulfillment" of Luke's earlier recorded prophecy from Jesus in Luke 21:12. Paul was slandered for Christ's sake, and that slander was part of what he understood to be persecution.

So, for example, Paul, speaking of himself and the other apostles, says, "When we are reviled, we bless; when we are persecuted, we endure; when we are slandered, we try to conciliate; we have become as the scum of the world, the dregs of all things, [even] until now" (1 Cor. 4:12–13). Paul has obviously been influenced by the instructions of Christ, as reflected here in

1 Corinthians 4 and in Romans 12:14 (see Matt. 5:44–48). Paul clearly knew persecution and sandwiched its mention between being reviled and being slandered. This mindset concerning slander and persecution makes sense if we treat seriously the words of Jesus, particularly taking into account the instruction attributed to him in Matthew.

One can see this same mindset exhibited by Peter, who says that one is blessed if he is reviled for the sake of Christ's name (1 Peter 4:14). The apostles clearly learned this from Jesus. Pobee does not consider whether or how Matthew 5:10–12 or 5:44–48 might have affected Paul's understanding of persecution. Neither does he include slander in the list of types of persecution found in the Pauline literature, but it certainly belongs. Though Pobee does speak of the Gospel accounts, he tends to view them as contributing to an overall Christological lens through which one might view Paul's preaching, rather than looking in the Gospels for accurate instructions on persecution from Jesus. Doesn't it seem likely that Paul would know of writings about Jesus? Is it not likely, then, that they might have influenced the development of his thoughts about persecution and martyrdom? It seems so. Paul was obviously well versed in the teachings of Jesus (see Acts 20:35).

Even more telling than these examples, however, is Pobee's neglect of 2 Timothy 3:12: "Moreover, all who want to live in a godly way in Christ Jesus will be persecuted."[5] Many scholars view 2 Timothy 3:12 as a foundational commentary by Paul on the topic of persecution. So, for instance, George Knight views this passage as "a general principle regarding persecution."[6] Luke Timothy Johnson refers to the verse as "a generalizing statement."[7] And Philip Towner sees the verse reflecting a "pattern of righteous suffering" that "encompasses the whole community of faith."[8] Towner develops the idea further and believes the verse to be integral to a proper understanding of not just persecution but of actual Christian existence. As he explains it, the persecution in view involves all Christians and in some way "normalizes" the experience of persecution.

---

5 Translation by Jerome D. Quinn and William C. Wacker, *The First and Second Letters to Timothy: A New Translation with Notes and Commentary* (Grand Rapids: Eerdmans, 1995), 744.

6 George W. Knight, *The Pastoral Epistles: A Commentary on the Greek Text* (Grand Rapids: Eerdmans, 1992), 440.

7 Luke Timothy Johnson, *The First and Second Letters to Timothy: A New Translation with Introduction and Commentary*, The Anchor Bible (New York: Doubleday, 2001), 422.

8 Philip Towner, *The Letters to Timothy and Titus* (Grand Rapids: Eerdmans, 2006), 577.

Whether one agrees with the assessment of these commentators or not is subordinate to the fact that their comments demonstrate the presence of a significant statement on persecution made by the apostle Paul. That Pobee does not discuss 2 Timothy 3:12 is peculiar. Whatever the explanation, the passage is foundational to Pauline theology regarding persecution, and his theology does not (at least on its surface) support Pobee's argument that persecution occurs as a manifestation of conflicting zeal. Rather, this passage speaks of a more basic origin for persecution.

Why will Christians face persecution? The answer from 2 Timothy 3:12 is not that Christians will be zealous and, thus, persecuted. Instead, Christians will face persecution because they *desire* to live devoted to Christ. It appears, then, that in Paul's writings persecution is inherently linked with allegiance to Christ. Being in Christ is enough to provoke persecution. Indeed, in 2 Timothy 3, Paul relates persecution to righteousness. For example, salvation is appropriated by faith in the Christ of Scripture (v. 15). Continuing in the faith through the Scriptures is called "training in righteousness" (v. 16).

Christ is the source of righteousness. So, Christ — his righteousness and rule — is the root cause of persecution against his followers (2 Tim. 3:12). From a biblical standpoint, this conclusion would not be surprising, considering that "this principle was already stated by Jesus (see Matt. 10:22–23; Luke 21:12; John 15:20) and by Paul, both on his first missionary journey (Acts 14:22) and in his earliest correspondence (1 Thess. 3:4)."[9] Of these last-mentioned verses, only the 1 Thessalonians passage is treated by Pobee. Yet, taken together, these verses affirm that allegiance to Christ is the sufficient condition for persecution because at root Christ is the one who provokes it.

One may object to this critique; perhaps the desire to live godly in Christ is what Pobee means by zeal. Pobee often makes zeal seem equal to being in relationship to Christ. For instance, he continually uses the term "devotee" as a descriptor of a Christian who expects persecution. But is a devotee necessarily zealous? Does devotion demand zeal, or might one be devoted and another be more zealous in his devotion? Devotion (or devotee) comports better than zeal regarding what we have seen throughout Scripture concerning the presence of Christ and persecution.

Elsewhere, Pobee wishes to preserve the distinction typically reserved

---

9 Knight, *The Pastoral Epistles,* 441.

in English for the notion of zeal, that is, a heightened intensity. So from the Maccabean tradition, he offers the example of Abraham and discusses how he is accepted by the Maccabean writers as a true martyr. Pobee argues that Abraham is a legitimate martyr, not because Abraham was faithful in the biblical sense (or righteous, as in Gen. 15:6 and Rom. 4:3), but because he demonstrated zeal in the legendary (apocryphal) account in which Nimrod threw him into a fiery furnace.

This legendary account is the one that Pobee accepts as the fully developed theology. According to this view, the typical understanding of Abraham's faith is inadequate as an explanation of persecution. What Pobee is saying here is that the Maccabean framework — the framework that he suggests provides the soil out of which Paul's theology grows — recognizes a distinction between being *righteous in Christ* and being *zealous for his cause*. On this distinction, the zealous Abraham is the Abraham who can be called a martyr. So Pobee does appear to hold a distinction between allegiance and zeal, and he argues that it is the latter that provokes persecution.

However, the declaration in 2 Timothy 3:12 makes no demand for zeal; rather, it simply asks for the believer to want godliness in Christ. In the context surrounding 2 Timothy 3:12, the contrasts are several: between what is true and false, between that which is evil and that which is godly, between those who follow the example of the world and those who follow after Christ (and thus become persecuted). There is no distinction made in the passage between lukewarm Christians and zealous ones. What Paul appears to be saying is not that those who are zealous (as opposed to those who are not) will be persecuted, but rather that those who desire to live godly in Christ (as opposed to those who do not) will be persecuted. Identification with Christ is enough to ensure persecution.

Going back to our Ghana story, Akua was outcast from her family not because she was overly zealous about her faith, but because she no longer identified herself as Muslim. When she trusted Christ, she rightly became identified with him. And the desire to identify with Christ was enough to force her to flee her home and family.

As our earlier study of Matthew and the Gospels proved, *Christ provokes the persecution*. His presence and his righteousness causes unbelievers to respond negatively. Confident that Paul was aware of the teachings of Christ, we conclude that Paul must be consistent with Jesus. Paul's assurance in

2 Timothy 3:12, then, that all who wish to live as followers of Christ Jesus will be persecuted is explained better by alliance with Christ than by zeal for his cause.

There are a number of practical reasons why our regnal righteousness approach to persecution makes better sense of the New Testament texts (particularly the Pauline texts) than does Pobee's explanation of zeal. First, zeal is not substantial enough to explain persecution. It is difficult to see how zeal by itself would cause Nazi leaders to chain Paul Schneider (the first Christian martyr in Nazi Germany) in a bowing position day after day. Why would zeal cause Akua's family to threaten, harass, and beat her? Zeal by itself might not be offensive. Zeal must take an object. The object, then, is the real cause of offense. Consider it this way: would Communists hunt down a man zealous for a fine cup of tea? Most likely not, even if he were obsessive about getting the perfect cup of this liquid concoction. Such a man would in all probability go unnoticed. Zeal takes an object. People are zealous for something or someone, zealous for a cause or for a movement. The person, the cause, the movement is the root element of offense.

The issue at its core is not the zeal but the object of the zeal. Pobee's thesis takes this critique into account by its assertion that persecution occurs as a manifestation of *conflicting* zeals. Thus he hopes to heighten the role of conflict. Even though he adds the element of conflict to further explain how zeal provokes persecution, still he leaves the most important question unasked. What is the root conflict? There may be two men in China who have conflicting zeals. Say, for instance, one man is zealous for his perfect cup of tea, the other zealous for the finest cup of coffee. China has a long history with tea. The second man is going against such history and "conflicting" with the zeal of the tea man. Surely, the man zealous for coffee is right in his zeal, but will he ever chain the tea man to the floor or try to kill him to make his point? Most likely not.

Zeals may, in fact, be in conflict without ever producing persecution. Zeal does not inherently provoke persecution any more than color inherently clashes with clothing. It is too generic. The zeals must be spelled out in order to know if there will be a clash, just as colors must be particularized before one can say they don't go together. Some shades of pink simply will neither coordinate with nor complement some shades of yellow. So too some zeals will neither cooperate with nor complement other zeals. The matter of conflict is decided not on the basis of the zeal itself, but on the more substantive root issue of the objects — or allegiances — in conflict.

Most often, this root issue of conflict is authority or power. Those under the authority and control of Christ, that is, those who are in allegiance to Christ, are a threat to the authority and power of others. To put the matter another way, those who live under the sovereignty of Christ in the kingdom of God will not always live in the same manner as those who abide in the "domain of darkness" (Col. 1:13). Zeal is not the substance of what brings about conflict between the two. Rather, the conflict is anchored in dominion. Who ultimately rules over people — Jesus or the prince of the power of the air? So to summarize the first point, zeal itself is not substantive enough to explain persecution.

Second, if we were to frame the matter of persecution in relation to zeal, then the question would arise as to whether zeal might be optional. Should Christians work to avoid persecution by simply not being so zealous? Indeed, this very scenario is on display throughout many Muslim and other hostile contexts today, giving rise to "underground" Christians who keep a low profile so as not to be noticed by their families or by authorities. Maybe Akua could have continued living in her family if she had been more discrete.

Some professing Christians attempt to temper their zeal so as not to bring about persecution. Yet even with their tempered zeal, they are often persecuted when their allegiance to Christ is exposed. Richard Wurmbrand's testimony is illustrative.[10] He was persecuted by the Communist government in Romania after claiming allegiance to Christ. He displayed no particular zeal in the beginning. He simply stated that his first allegiance was to Christ and not Communism. Granted, from a Communist perspective, the "not Communism" aspect of Wurmbrand's decision might have been enough for him to head to prison. A great number of non-Christians were imprisoned for not supporting Communism. Yet, as Wurmbrand bore witness, his action was driven by faith in Christ. Insofar as he could be both Christian and Communist, he was willing. His action was not taken against Communism as much as it was for Christ. For that he was imprisoned and routinely persecuted for fourteen years. The point is, Christians ought to be wise and

---

10 Richard Wurmbrand, *Tortured for Christ* (Bartlesville, OK: Living Sacrifice Book Company, 1967).

cautious, but even with their attempts at discretion, ought to expect persecution — not because they are zealous but because they belong to Christ, whose authority is perceived as a threat to all other powers. Zealous or not, those wishing to follow Christ are subject to persecution, as Paul writes in 2 Timothy 3:12.

So to answer the question concerning whether Christians ought to avoid persecution by tempering their zeal, the reply is that, in wisdom, Christians ought to demonstrate prudence and caution, but they will not by such efforts avoid persecution. Persecution is not rooted as much in their degree of devotion as it is in their identification with Christ.

Third, there is a history of equating zeal with *zealotism*, in which those who are zealots are viewed negatively by the social community. Rome, in the century in which Paul was writing, certainly had a particular distaste for zealots. And some zealots, as Paul himself testified in Philippians 3:6, had a particular distaste for Christians. Such zealotism did, in fact, increase the likelihood of conflicts, particularly since the zealots were often characterized by violence. The Christian ought to be careful about setting up expectations of zeal with respect to persecution and martyrdom. Whereas the apostle Paul would through faith in Christ cry out, "I die daily," he was not willing to kill for his cause. He did not advocate killing or violence in his devotion to Christ. Where zealots were characterized by their willingness both to die and to kill, Paul was characterized by teaching Christians how to live in peace with others — even with those who might persecute them (see Rom. 8:6; 12:18; 14:19; 1 Cor. 7:15; 14:33; 2 Cor. 13:11; Col. 3:15; 1 Thess. 5:13).

The apostle Paul viewed zeal both positively and negatively. Paul was pleased with the Corinthian zeal that came from godly sorrow (2 Cor. 7:11). Yet, Paul also recognized that the zeal of the Jews was not in accordance with knowledge (Rom. 10:2). And Paul went so far as to say that there is a zeal that is a manifestation of the flesh (Gal. 5:20). Zeal can also be a mark of godliness (as in 2 Cor. 11:2). Again, the object of zeal must be considered in determining whether zeal is positive or negative. Pobee might adjust his thesis just a bit to say that persecution (rather than being a sure sign) is more likely in contexts where Christians are zealous for Christ. Zeal may increase the likelihood that the Christian will be noticed, but it does not initiate the provocation to persecution.

Pobee's statements about Paul's having persecuted Christians because of his zeal for the law betray his conclusion that persecution is rooted in zeal. It is not. Before Paul came to Christ, the spirit of persecution was rooted in his allegiance to Jewish traditions that were threatened by Christ. Christ himself was the root issue, which explains why Luke's conversion narrative in Acts 9 has Christ asking Paul, "Why are you persecuting *me*?" Elsewhere, Pobee acknowledges the very point being made here, that "Paul interpreted the persecutions he underwent as evidence that he was a devotee of Christ and of God."[11] The presence of persecution, then, is a sure sign in Pauline theology of the presence of Christ. Those desiring to live as Christians are persecuted. From our review thus far, we can affirm the following observations:

- While zeal might increase the probability of persecution, it does not define persecution.
- The conflict of persecution is a conflict between allegiance to Christ and allegiance to other worldly authorities.
- Our understanding of persecution should be shaped mostly by the Old Testament, the New Testament, and Jesus himself.
- Persecution, including slanders and insults, is possible for any follower of Christ.
- Zeal itself does not provoke persecution; rather, the object of zeal — Christ — provokes persecution.

How do these observations and conclusions square with the rest of Paul's teaching? Paul, having composed more than a dozen New Testament books, wrote extensively on the topic of persecution. Beyond understanding the subject theologically and biblically, Paul obviously experienced a great deal of persecution personally. He puts himself in the persecution equation on an experiential basis. Persecution is not just a subject for academic study. For him, persecution is "filling up what is lacking in Christ's afflictions for the sake of his body, that is, the church" (Col. 1:24 ESV). For Paul, it is personal.

Just how personal for Paul is a bit of a controversy. When Paul says that he is filling up what is lacking in Christ's suffering, is he saying that the atoning work of Christ is incomplete and must be finished by those who suffer persecution? To explain the difficulty of this passage, scholars have landed

---

11   Wurmbrand, *Tortured for Christ*, 94.

in one of three interpretations on this passage, called *atoning, mystical,* or *eschatological* (meaning related to the end-times).

Almost unanimously, scholars have rejected the first option. The reason the atonement option is rejected is simple. Paul does not believe anyone needs to do any work to add to the saving work of Christ. He wrote emphatically against such thinking elsewhere (Eph. 2:5, 8–10). Paul does not appear to say that suffering persecution earns merit toward salvation.

In fact, the language Paul uses in the Colossians passage is more like the language we discussed in Acts: it's the language of tribulation and suffering various trials, not the language of sacrificial suffering on the cross. In Acts, we saw that Paul's own conversion started with the revelation of Christ identifying with his persecuted church (Acts 9). Elsewhere, Paul makes plain that present sufferings are tied to (and not worthy to be compared with) the future revelation of Christ (Rom. 8:18). So the better explanation for Paul's meaning is found somewhere between the other two interpretation options. The "filling up" of what is lacking in Christ's suffering is either an indication of personally identifying with Christ (mystical), or so closely identifying with him in his eternal mission that the incidents of persecution are related to the ultimate plan of redemption accomplished over time through Christ (eschatological).

Persecution in Paul's writings is personal and is intimately connected with Christ as his eternal mission unfolds. While Paul himself was zealous and encouraged the churches to be zealous, he did not connect such zeal with persecution. Instead, persecution was related to the desire to live godly in Christ. Persecution happened in the churches because of Christ. Much of what Paul wrote, he penned so that churches like the one in Thessalonica might continue in steadfastness and faith in all the persecutions and afflictions they suffered. Again, Paul both affirms the view of persecution we have seen thus far and adds his own unique perspective to the conversation, that is, it fills up what is lacking in Christ's body.

8

THE BOOK OF HEBREWS:

A CALL TO REMEMBER THE PERSECUTED

Remember the prisoners, as though in prison with them,
and those who are ill-treated, since you yourselves also
are in the body.

(Heb. 13:3)

I recently read the story of a man who practiced his craft hour after hour, day after day. He trained with his rifle until his nerves were unaffected by firing shot after shot into the blackened head of the human silhouette on his target some distance away. He honed his skills so he could sneak into homes unnoticed, as quietly as a black cat stalking her prey.

On this particular night, he entered the target home, crept silently from room to room, and traversed the stairway with ease, inspecting room after room, until he reached his goal in an upstairs bedroom. Having practiced so often on the darkened silhouette, he had no problem hitting his man with multiple shots to the head.

A second man I read about was nowhere near as crafty as the first. He knew how to use a gun, and so in that limited sense he was trained. But he had no genuine skill as a marksman. As crude as he was, he too was able to subdue his target. His ability to scamper cat-like through a house was neither perfected nor necessary. He only needed to make it into the living room on the main floor of the house, where his subject lay fast asleep. Once he reached his destination, the shots were fired and the deadly deed was done.

How should we assess these actions? Are these men cold-blooded murderers? Surely that appears to be the case for what does premeditated murder look like if not like this? As it turns out, however, the first subject is a national hero; the second, a murderous low-life. The difference between the two is not in their actions, but in the context defining their actions.

The first man was on a mission of national security. And he succeeded. He has been awarded military honors, including the Silver Star. At least three feature films have been made depicting his actions as both heroic and courageous. He is the featured character in *Zero Dark Thirty, Captain Phillips,* and *Lone Survivor.* He is Navy Seal hero Rob O'Neill, the man who killed Osama bin Laden.

The second subject is largely unknown, a troubled teenager from Florida, who killed his grandfather with whom he had been living in northwest Orange County. Oakley Miller, who was 19 when he killed his grandfather Donald Gonnelly, has been found guilty of second-degree murder (in a plea bargain) and sentenced to twenty-five years in prison for his actions. Ostensibly, each of these men did the same thing: armed themselves, entered a home, and shot their subjects repeatedly. Outward behavior was much the same. But we rightly make distinctions between these killings: one was a crime against humanity, the other an act of war.

The contrast between these two killings illustrates an important point for understanding the nature of biblical commands. Commands in the Bible are theologically contained. The Bible is not like a student handbook or a hospital employee's code of conduct. The Bible is revelation from God for his people. Thus the commands are explained theologically. For believers, the commands of Scripture always concern God and God's people. Consider a few examples.

Both Saul (Israel's inaugural king) and Abel (humanity's first murder victim — and martyr) offered meat sacrificed to God. In the case of Abel, God was pleased. Abel was counted righteous, which instigated persecution against him by Cain, who had to be rebuked by God for his seething unrighteousness. By contrast, in the case of Saul, God was not pleased. In fact, God was so displeased with Saul that he declared the kingdom would be removed from him and given to another (1 Sam. 13:12–14). Each man offered meat in a sacrifice to God. Why did God react so differently to the two men, affirming one and condemning the other?

The distinction hinges on the relationship between God and his people. God, we learn, delights in obedience, not in sacrifice: "And Samuel said, 'Has the LORD as great delight in burnt offerings and sacrifices, as in obeying the voice of the LORD? Behold, to obey is better than sacrifice, and to listen than the fat of rams'" (1 Sam. 15:22 ESV). Saul had been commanded to wait but he would not. Biblical commands are always theologically contained.

Consider a couple of New Testament examples. Peter writes, "But as he who called you is holy, you also be holy in all your conduct, since it is written, 'You shall be holy, for I am holy'" (1 Peter 1:15–16 ESV). The command is a direct reflection of relationship to God. Strictly speaking, this command has more to do with relationship than with any particular moral action. Such a relational dynamic is ubiquitous throughout the Scriptures. So the apostle John tells his readers, "Beloved, if God so loved us, we ought also to love one another" (1 John 4:11). The pattern is clear. God is the reference point of biblical commands. Obedience is meant both for theology and for community. Notice the central role of relationship.

With that pattern in mind, we turn our attention to the command found in Hebrews 13:3, "Remember the prisoners, as though in prison with them, and those who are ill-treated, since you yourselves also are in the body." The command itself is simple enough: *remember*! The command is a plural imperative, meaning that it is a command given to the group of believers. The readers in mind were apparently in danger of drifting away from the faith (see 6:9–12). So the command was originally for the church to remember those being persecuted on account of Christ. In fact, this command could have been encouraging these Christians to "continue remembering" the persecuted (as they had been doing previously; 10:32–35). Either way, the command fits the pattern we have seen above — conditioned on God and Christian community. The command is theologically contained. God expects his people to identify with their own family of faith, providing care for them. To say it another way, when times get tough for God's people, God expects his people to come together, not to drift away.

Textually, however, a problem arises when we look further at the reason given for our remembering. We expect that the above explanation would suffice, but the phrase at the end of Hebrews 13:3 creates some difficulty. What is the reason Christians are to remember? The answer to that question is found in the final phrase of 13:3, which is translated variously as follows:

"since you also are in the body" (ESV)

"since you yourselves also are in the body" (NASB)

"as if you yourselves were suffering" (NIV)

"as if you felt their pain in your own bodies" (NLT)

"as being yourselves also in the body" (KJV)

Obviously, these translations reflect slight variations in the meaning of this final phrase. Three translations focus on "the body," while the two more dynamic translations (NLT, NIV) give attention to bodily suffering in general. So why are Christians commanded to remember the persecuted? Is it because we also are in the body (of Christ), or is it because we are likewise in a body prone to suffering as they are? Most often, Christians understand the verse to mean in the body of Christ. So, for instance, Voice of the Martyrs uses this verse as their foundation for ministering to persecuted Christians around the world. The idea is that Christians should remember those who are persecuted because all Christians are one body in Christ.

New Testament scholars, however, interpret the phrase along the lines of the dynamic translations. So, Paul Ellingworth states, "There is no reference to the church as Christ's body, as Calvin thought."[1] Regardless of what Calvin might have thought, of course, we must wrestle with Scripture itself to determine what the text is saying. What is the motivation given in Hebrews 13:3 for remembering our persecuted brothers and sisters in the faith?

The difficulty of interpreting the text stems from two sources. First, we bring certain ideas to the text, forgetting that these texts were written in the first century, long before the Christian church had time to clarify properly every point of its theology. In other words, we read these texts today from the perspective of all we have learned through centuries of Christian writers. It is, therefore, quite natural for Christians today to speak of the church as the body of Christ.

---

1 Paul Ellingworth, *The Epistle to the Hebrews: A Commentary on the Greek Text*, NIGTC (Grand Rapids: Eerdmans, 1993), 696.

However, that language comes mostly from Paul (1 Cor. 12, for instance). We cannot be sure that the first readers of Hebrews had access to Paul's writings. Perhaps they would not have immediately identified "the body" as the body of Christ. Thus, scholars warn us to avoid importing our ideas into the text. We should take the text at face value and learn from it according to the meaning it had for the author and his audience.

That being said, then, the second source of difficulty is the text itself. In the original Greek, there is no definite article. In other words, "the" in the phrase "in *the* body" does not technically exist. It is provided in translation. No one is engaging in chicanery here. All translations must provide words to bring ideas from one language system into another. Scholars note, however, that the final phrase of Hebrews 13:3 could be more accurately translated as "being yourselves in *a* body." Like Ellingworth, they are saying that our tendency to supply "the" is a result of our being influenced by the apostle Paul's teaching on the church as the body of Christ.

Obviously, we want our theology and our actions to be built on what God's Word says, not on what we want it to say. We should be thankful for scholars who constantly remind us that faith is nurtured by the texts that God has preserved in the Scriptures. As the scholars note, we must decide from the text how to understand the final phrase of Hebrews 13:3. Most scholars say to understand it not as "the body of Christ" but as "being in a body too." The idea would be, remember the persecuted because you too suffer in bodily form. You too can relate to their pain, their weakness, their vulnerability. You too may in fact find yourself suffering with them in prison someday. So identify with them now as though you are with them.

We can understand why scholars translate the text the way they do. I recognize the need to sympathize with suffering saints. However, I do not believe this interpretation gets at the heart of the message of Hebrews. To me, such an interpretation would be seriously anticlimactic. It would be like saying, "My wife is in prison, and I should remember her because I could end up in prison one day too." Something is wrong with that logic. The writer of Hebrews has been relentlessly imploring readers to identify with Christ, to remember him who is their high priest, to consider him, to stir up one another in love, to continue meeting together faithfully. Why would he then abandon this radical call to Christian identity and urge them in chapter 13 to remember the persecuted because they too share in the frailties of the human condition?

The command to remember in Hebrews 13:3 sounds less like a command of sympathy and more like a command of empathy — calling the reader to identify fully with these persecuted brothers and sisters. I readily admit that scholars smarter than I am (e.g., Ellingworth) suggest that my view is incorrect. My aim, like theirs, is simply to accept by faith what the text of the Bible teaches. In support of my opinion, I offer the following five observations, which point to an interpretation along the lines of the ESV and the NASB, even allowing for the text to mean *the* body of Christ.

Five Observations for Interpreting Hebrews 13:3

First, the writer of Hebrews is radically centered on Christ and the church. As a pastor, I once preached a series through the book of Hebrews that took four years. Week after week, we listened to this writer as he lifted Christ high above us and told us over and over again to think of Christ, consider him, fix our eyes on him. The book has the vibe of a pastor pleading with Christians to come together in unity under the headship of the Great Shepherd of the sheep. Not surprisingly, the book addresses its audience in the first-person plural ("we" and "us") more than fifty times — that's an average of four such references for each chapter. A perfect example of this "we" dynamic is on display in the book's statement of its main purpose: "Now the main point in what has been said is this: *we* have such a high priest, who has taken His seat at the right hand of the throne of the Majesty in the heavens" (Heb. 8:1; emphasis mine). The writer is pleading for Christians to realize the glory of this resurrection reality — that we have a high priest who endures with divine power. The "we" is an unmistakable declaration that Christ lives for his church (see 7:24–26). Ultimately, the writer of Hebrews reflects the tendency found in all the Bible to focus attention on God at work in the midst of his people.

Second, Hebrews 13:3 (in the Greek text) has a parallel structure.

Remember those in prison . . . as though in prison <u>with them,</u>
and those who are mistreated . . . being in a body _____

The Greek text only says "being in a body." The writer assumed the thought would be concluded by the reader. How should we complete the thought? As noted above, many scholars fill in the blank with "like them." Thus the thought would be "since you are in bodily form like them." But the parallel seems to work better in this sentence if we finish the thought "with them." The first part of the sentence calls for close identification with the prisoners — as though being bound *with* them. So too the second part of the sentence calls for close identification *with* those who are ill-treated: being in a body with them.

Third, chapter 13 is the conclusion of a robust theology focused on Christ as the high priest for his followers. Christ's work on behalf of the church should lead Christians toward a pattern of also working on behalf of the church. To borrow a line from John, "Whoever says he abides in him ought to walk in the same way in which he walked" (1 John 2:6 ESV).

As we noted in the beginning of this chapter, commands are expressions of a relationship with God. Christian life and thought are shaped by Christ himself. Hebrews 13 offers many commands and injunctions — but only after the first twelve chapters of the book have explained thoroughly how Jesus walked before his people in order to accomplish salvation. As a result, we ought to walk in a manner worthy of Christ. How then do we do this? The first verse in Hebrews 13 spells it out: "Let brotherly love continue." The significance of Christians using family terms like "brother" to describe their close relation to one another is summed up nicely by Ellingworth and Nida:

> At that time it was rare for the word "brother" to be used in speaking of those who were not members of the same family, or at least of the same ethnic group. In the Old Testament, "brother" in its widest sense meant "fellow-Israelite" (Lev. 19:17–18; Acts 13:26). Christians thought of themselves as members of the same family, whether or not they were physically related. So "brotherly love" is not love which is merely like the love of brothers . . . but the love of those who were truly, though not physically, related in the Christian "brotherhood."[2]

So brotherly love in the first verse has significance for the third verse and the author's admonition to remember brothers and sisters suffering for their faith. Such remembering is a Christian family affair.

---

2   Paul Ellingworth and E. A. Nida, *A Handbook on the Letter to the Hebrews* (New York: United Bible Societies, 1994), 320.

The fourth reason to understand verse 3 to be speaking of identification with the suffering body of Christ is the history of this congregation with persecution. These believers were part of a congregation who had already suffered persecution. Perhaps, the persecution they suffered was the persecution instigated in Rome by Emperor Claudius (AD 49). This congregation embraced the suffering with triumphant joy on account of Christ (10:32–34). George Guthrie gets to the heart of the congregation's faith: "The hearers had joy in the midst of their persecution because they knew that 'better and lasting possessions' were promised them by virtue of their identification with the Lord and his church."[3] As Guthrie demonstrates, the strength of the congregation is its identification both with the Lord and with his church. In many ways, the author of Hebrews views these as inseparable realities.

The congregation already knew persecution, and they already understood how persecution relates to Christ and his church. As chapter 10 makes plain, the congregation had not only suffered persecution, but they had "become sharers" with others in the congregation through their suffering. This concept of sharing represents the New Testament idea of fellowship, that is, a partnership between those who take part in a great cause with others likewise committed. They were partners, companions in gospel ministry. Because they had already suffered persecution together, they would likely have understood the command in 13:3 to be a return to their former mentality, much like the admonition from chapter 10. This command, then, could have been personal and congregational.

Finally, the fifth reason to understand Hebrews 13:3 as calling for identification with the body of Christ is the fact that such body language is not as foreign to the writer of Hebrews as some may think. The author of Hebrews is not the apostle Paul. Paul spent a great deal of time defending his apostleship on the basis that Christ revealed himself to Paul, even if it were as to one as untimely born (1 Cor. 15:8). Thus, it is not likely that Paul would then consider himself as a second-generation believer. The writer of Hebrews says that he got the word in the second generation from the original apostles (2:3).

Of course, the writer of Hebrews could have been well acquainted with Paul. If the author were Apollos, for instance, then he would have been well

---

3   George Guthrie, *Hebrews*, The NIV Application Commentary (Grand Rapids: Zondervan, 1998), 359.

versed in Paul's teaching (1 Cor. 3:6–9; Titus 3:13). Thus the writer of Hebrews could have been familiar with the concept of the body used as a metaphor for Christ's church. More to the point, though, this writer actually uses body metaphors in 12:12–16 to encourage this church to persevere by faith:

> Therefore lift your drooping hands and strengthen your weak knees, and make straight paths for your feet, so that what is lame may not be put out of joint but rather be healed. Strive for peace with everyone, and for the holiness without which no one will see the Lord. See to it that no one fails to obtain the grace of God; that no "root of bitterness" springs up and causes trouble, and by it many become defiled; that no one is sexually immoral or unholy like Esau, who sold his birthright for a single meal. (ESV)

In the passage, the church is exhorted to be holy (v. 14). The author is serious about holiness — so much so that he calls each one in the church to look out for the other, making sure that no member of the church falls away. He also calls the church to watch out so that no one falls to the temptation of sexual immorality (v. 16). In his zeal for the holiness of the church, this writer defaults to several allusions to human anatomy. In verse 12, he encourages them to lift drooping hands and strengthen weak knees. In the following verse, the church is to keep the way clear so their feet will stay on the narrow path. Whatever is wrong in the church (whatever limb is lame) must be cared for so that the church is not put out of joint but rather healed.

We shouldn't overstate the case, but we can insist from this passage in chapter 12 that speaking of the church as a body is not a completely foreign concept for this writer. The command in 13:3 is not too far removed from this admonition for the church to be a united body mutually encouraging one another to holiness for the sake of Christ. I think the writer of Hebrews desires for Christians to think of the church as a body that needs strengthening and encouragement through seasons of persecution for the sake of holiness.

Our conclusion, then, from this brief summary of persecution in the book of Hebrews is that the book links believers to God through Christ. The commands of the book — including the command to remember the persecuted — are built from a theological context. The commands are about relationship between God and his people. Thus in Hebrews 13:3, the context is familial love (13:1), which should lead this congregation to remember their Christian family for the sake of Christ and holiness.

Further, going back to our discussion of the regnal dynamic in Matthew, we can still see the Christ-righteousness framework in Hebrews, even if the language is different. In Hebrews, the stress is on sanctification (as in 12:12–14). Yet the idea of sanctification (or holiness) in Hebrews is not totally dissimilar to the concept of righteousness in Matthew. Both books are likely drawing from Isaiah's concept of preparing the way of the Lord. Because Christ has been raised up, exalted by God to the heavenly places, he is now working to bring his people to himself, setting us apart in holiness/righteousness.

Persecution in Hebrews, like persecution in Matthew, highlights both Christ and his people. Believers are set apart by Christ as the church. The unity of believers under the headship of Christ is a primary emphasis of the book of Hebrews, and thus is an integral factor in what is said about persecution. Christians ought to love Christians for the sake of Christ. To love is to remember. So Christians are to remember those who are ill-treated, being ourselves in a body with them.

9

PETER'S EPISTLES:
PERSECUTION AND THE BLESSED LIFE

If you are insulted for the name of Christ, you are blessed,
because the Spirit of glory and of God rests upon you.
(1 Peter 4:14 ESV)

My friend and I both agreed that we were blessed. There we were, sitting on a picturesque beach in a remote village far away from the crowded streets of Davao City, the premier city in the southern Philippines. The nearest Starbucks was about 800 miles away. In front of us were gently rolling waves of azure blue, topped with thin ribbons of whitened foam providing an outline to trace each wave as it glided effortlessly onto shore. Still sparkling by the light of the evening sun, the blue water established a stable foreground against the backdrop of a deep pink and orange-striped sky that illumined this portion of the Pacific Ocean better than a team of Hollywood lighting designers could. Looking out over the Davao Gulf, we watched the multicolored spectacle of a Filipino outrigger — white canopy top contrasting with the primary red, blue, and yellow hull — as it jostled its way steadily over the sea, past the tree-lined, green hills of Sigaboy Island and onward into the Philippine Sea.

We were blessed also because in front of us was a perfect array of the world's freshest fruit. On the weathered white table nearest the sea was an orange bowl filled with small, yellow bananas — bananas with a sweetness so intense they seemed artificial. And better than the bananas were the Asian mangoes, which grow more delicious on Mindanao Island than anywhere in the world. The pale, yellow skin covers the deep golden flesh of the mangoes, which taste more like yellow cling peaches in heavy syrup than they do a typical, store-bought mango in America. The fruit was amazing. Yet the fruit was there merely to supplement the endless supply of fresh calamari and tuna. We were so blessed to be where we were.

The greatest blessing, however, was not this sensory cornucopia in front of us, but what was behind us. Behind the fruit, the seafood, and the sea were the dozens of tribal and village pastors who had traveled down from remote mountain villages to hear the Word of God. We were there to preach and teach — to train these pastors as they continued to shepherd their flocks to the glory of God. These pastors were gathered for encouragement and edification. We traveled halfway around the world to be with them, to enjoy the food, and — even better — to share fellowship in Christ.

With these Christian brothers, we mined the treasures of wisdom and knowledge revealed in Christ and preserved in the Scriptures. We were blessed indeed to be gathered with these saints and servants. Ironically, though, a debate broke out among the group — and between me and my pastor friend — when someone questioned the meaning of being "blessed." While experiencing God's blessing, we debated the meaning of being "blessed."

The debate erupted when we began exploring the New Testament teaching on Christian persecution. Can the persecuted be called blessed? Some did not think so. No one hesitated to call the sea and the beach a blessing. There was no hesitation to add the mangoes, bananas, and calamari to the list of blessings from God. All of us agreed that the fellowship we shared was a greater blessing than eating well while looking across the sea. But we could not all say that suffering persecution at the hands of evil men should be called the blessed life.

Tension rises when we consider the teaching of the New Testament authors. Already, we've seen how plainly Matthew states the relation between blessing and persecution:

> Blessed are those who are persecuted for righteousness' sake, for theirs is the kingdom of heaven. Blessed are you when others revile you and persecute you and utter all kinds of evil against you falsely on my account. Rejoice and be glad, for your reward is great in heaven, for so they persecuted the prophets who were before you. (Matt. 5:10–12 ESV)

Matthew is not alone. Luke says Christians should leap for joy when people hate them and spurn their name as evil (Luke 6:22–23). Not coincidentally, Luke also says that Peter and John did rejoice exceedingly when they were counted worthy to suffer for the name of Christ (Acts 5:41). Likewise, James says that Christians should count it all joy when the fiery trials of persecution come upon them, even saying that the "blessed" Christian is the one who endures such trials faithfully (James 1:2, 12). After calling Christians to endurance, John says that those who die in faith are blessed (Rev. 14:13).

But of all the New Testament writers, Peter is perhaps the most vocal about the blessing of persecution. His statement in 1 Peter 4:14 forces us to grapple with the seemingly incompatible concepts of *blessing* and *persecution*: "If you are insulted for the name of Christ, you are blessed, because the Spirit of glory and of God rests upon you" (ESV).

Like the other New Testament writers, Peter doesn't view the Christian's suffering as an anomaly. Early in this letter, Peter encourages his readers to persevere through their trials, knowing that the outcome will be a purifying of the pure gold of their faith that will, in turn, glorify Christ (1 Peter 1:6–7). In chapter 3, Peter reminds these believers that no one is able to harm them if they are upright before the Lord. He further encourages them, "But even if you should suffer for righteousness' sake, you will be blessed. Have no fear of them, nor be troubled" (v. 14 ESV). Sounding like Matthew, Peter encourages his audience to do what is right for Christ's sake. It may cost them comfort, convenience, and safety, but the gain of Christ is more than adequate compensation for whatever is lost. Peter and the other New Testament writers agree on this point.

Yet Peter extends the conversation beyond merely expecting persecution. For Peter, Christians should suffer well, and if they do, they will in fact be living the blessed life of a believer in Jesus Christ.

Peter forces us to struggle with the notion of a persecuted life being called the blessed life. Has Peter manufactured some pathological, masochistic vision of Christian living in the name of a crucified Messiah? No. Peter is simply sober-minded about living as a Christian in a world opposed to Christ (see 1 Peter 3:18–4:11). Living the blessed life in Christ may include suffering through seasons of persecution.

In his helpful guide to 1 Peter, Greg Forbes outlines from 1 Peter 4:12–14 three aspects of blessing in relation to persecution.[1] According to Forbes, verse 12 indicates "that suffering is to be expected"; verse 13 shows "that a proper attitude to suffering will result in even greater rejoicing"; and verse 14 relates to cause, "showing the reason why believers are blessed when reviled for the name of Christ." This three-part breakdown by Forbes is helpful in shaping the outlook a Christian might hold toward persecution and blessing. These three aspects can be understood as the *end*, the *ethic*, and the *essence* of persecution.

Peter's Three Aspects of Persecution

The first aspect (v. 12) outlines the *end* of suffering from Peter's perspective. Suffering has a point. Of course, the point could be many different things. Perhaps suffering is a form of punishment. Or suffering could be a kind of proving ground to see whether a professing Christian is genuinely a Christian. Perhaps suffering is designed to fit Christians for their later ruling and reigning with Christ.[2] What does suffering prove?

Forbes argues that suffering proves faith; it is a trial that burns away the dross and leaves the pure gold of Christian integrity. In this sense, then, the believer should not be surprised that such refining work comes upon him from God. As Christ's people go forth in the world, they become targets of the unbeliever's hostility toward God. But God has a redemptive purpose in such suffering. As Forbes puts it, "Unbelievers are surprised at the behavior of Christians, but Christians are not surprised at the behavior of unbelievers toward them."[3] Christians will suffer, but never in vain.

Peter teaches believers that the end of suffering far exceeds the mean aim of those inflicting it. Unbelievers may in fact act with great hostility toward believers, but the end of the matter will be settled by God, who intends the suffering to accomplish a good end. New Testament scholar Thomas

---

1   Greg Forbes, *1 Peter*, Exegetical Guide to the Greek New Testament (Nashville: B & H Academic, 2014), 152–53.

2   Josef Ton, *Suffering, Martyrdom, and Rewards in Heaven* (Wheaton, IL: The Romanian Missionary Society, 2000). Such a view of suffering is difficult to separate from works-based salvation, on the one hand, and a diminishing of Christ on the other.

3   Forbes, *1 Peter*, 153.

Schreiner captures the essence of Peter's end goal for suffering: "This notion is standard in New Testament paraenesis, for God uses the trials of life to strengthen the character of believers and to make them fit for his presence (see Rom. 5:3–5; James 1:2–4)."[4] This end goal of suffering is a challenge to believers, reminding us that even though we have believed in Jesus and have received life in his name, we still are far from the final glorified state he has purposed for us. God uses trials to fit us for eternal life in his presence (the final blessed state).

The second aspect (v. 13) is the *ethic* of suffering persecution. What ought a Christian do when persecution strikes? Rejoice, of course! K. H. Jobes offers keen insight that captures Peter's point:

> If suffering for Christ should be the believer's experience, Peter reframes it as a reason not for bitterness or despair but for joy (4:13). The thought that suffering produces joy is as strange as Peter's earlier statement that those who suffer are "blessed" (3:14). This does not mean that the believer should enjoy suffering per se, but undeserved suffering because of Christian faith is evidence of future eschatological deliverance, which will bring the ultimate joy a human being can experience.[5]

Strictly speaking, the suffering itself does not produce the joy. The joy is a responsive action. Peter commands his readers to rejoice. Rejoicing is the ethic — how the Christian ought to respond to the fiery trial of persecution. That being said, Jobes's remarks get to the heart of Peter's message: *suffering persecution has a blessing built into it.* The command to rejoice may have sounded as strange to the first-century reader as it does to the postmodern American reader. And yet, Peter and the New Testament writers expect such a command to somehow make sense to believers. In what way could it make sense to rejoice in response to being persecuted? Jobes hints that persecution is a down payment on the ultimate deliverance for which God's people are waiting. Notice how Peter anchors these verses in the present as well as in

---

4   Thomas R. Schreiner, *1, 2 Peter, Jude*, The New American Commentary 37 (Nashville: Broadman & Holman, 2003), 219. "Paraenesis" is moral advice or exhortation a philosopher would offer his pupils.

5   K. H. Jobes, *1 Peter*, Baker Exegetical Commentary on the New Testament (Grand Rapids: Baker, 2005), 287.

the future: "But rejoice insofar as you share Christ's sufferings, that you may also rejoice and be glad when his glory is revealed. If you are insulted for the name of Christ, you are blessed, because the Spirit of glory and of God rests upon you" (1 Peter 4:13–14 ESV).

The first part of these verses is written in the present tense: rejoice now insofar as you are sharing in Christ's suffering. Then the future goal is established, so that you also will rejoice and be glad when Christ returns and our full glorification unfolds. This back-and-forth pattern from present to future speaks of the Christian's participation in the "already/not yet" of the kingdom of God. We are already partakers of Christ, yet we've only just begun to live in him. And we have not yet realized the full glory of life in his presence. The reality of redemption and eternity will unfold yet another dramatic layer of deliverance for us from the flesh and from this world's corruption. In the meantime, however, believers are living the blessed life when insulted for the name of Christ. Peter says the reason that this is the blessed life is "because the Spirit of glory and of God" rests upon the saint who suffers for Christ. Rejoice when persecuted because the Spirit of glory and of God is upon you.

This conversation concerning the ethic of rejoicing leads inevitably to the necessary consideration of Forbes's third aspect: the *essence* of the blessedness of persecution. If our exploration of these three aspects reflects accurately Peter's intentions, then the *end* of persecution is purification for God's presence; the *ethic* of persecution is rejoicing now in his presence (and later at Christ's consummation); and the *essence* of persecution is a blessed life. The challenge we've come to now sits in sharp focus. It's the same challenge we debated on the beach: how is persecution a blessing?

Blessed Because of the Spirit of Glory and of God

The first note to sound on the matter of blessing is that it should ring untrue when we hear someone say that persecution is a blessing. Technically, persecution is not called a blessing. Rather, those who suffer persecution are called blessed. The distinction may seem insignificant, but it reflects a profound biblical priority. Where we tend to count possessions as "blessings," thus thinking the one with the most blessings is consequently the most blessed, the Bible speaks instead of blessing existing in relation to God. People are blessed who dwell in harmony with God. Those who experience the favorable presence of God are blessed. If we think of the word "happy," which is how some have translated the word "blessed," then we can understand the distinction Peter and other New Testament writers are making. To be happy is to be in a state of bliss or exuberant joy. Certain possessions may facilitate being in that state, but they do not themselves consist of happiness. So it is with being blessed. Persecution is not the blessing, but it may facilitate the blessed state of dwelling harmoniously in the presence of God.

As Peter says, suffering persecution on account of Christ is a clear indication that one is experiencing the Spirit of God. Peter appears to be saying that to be persecuted is to be blessed "because the Spirit of glory and of God" rests upon the suffering saint.

Naturally, the next question is what Peter means that the Spirit of glory and of God rests on the persecuted. Scholars have differing opinions about who or what is the spirit (Spirit) of glory and of God. Some (like Jobes) believe the phrase speaks of empowerment to endure persecution. Others think the phrase is a foretaste of the future glorification of the saints in the presence of Christ. Peter Davids makes the compelling case that this phrase refers to nothing less than the presence of God. For Davids, this Spirit of glory and of God

> is what Jesus promised in Matthew 10:19–20, "When they deliver you up . . . for what you are to say will be given you in that hour; for it is not you who speak, but the Spirit of your Father speaking through you" (Mark 13:11; Luke 12:11–12). Stephen experienced the glory of God in his martyrdom (Acts 7:55; he was, of course, a man full of the Spirit, 6:15), and so would other martyrs later. . . . Thus those suffering for Christ experience through the Spirit now the glory they are promised in the future (1:7; 5:4; see 2 Cor. 4:17; Col. 3:4). Indeed, their very suffering is a sign that the reputation (glory) of God is seen in them, that the Spirit rests upon them. They can indeed count themselves blessed.[6]

---

6 Peter Davids, *The First Epistle of Peter*, The New International Commentary on the New Testament (Grand Rapids: Eerdmans, 1990), 168.

In the earlier chapter on the Gospel of Matthew, we saw the relation between the presence of Christ and persecution. Thus it comes as no surprise to find Peter restating a similar relationship here. As in Matthew, the presence of Christ is the key to understanding the blessedness of persecution. Peter, of course, speaks of the presence of God rather than of Christ, but divine presence is the key.

The main point of verse 14 is that the person who suffers for Christ is blessed. Schreiner clarifies the point this way: "[Christians] may be insulted by human beings, but they are blessed by God himself."[7] This truth — that suffering saints are blessed by God himself — solves the riddle of the persecution blessing: *God himself is the blessing.* He is present with his people who suffer on account of him. Again, Schreiner offers a clarifying word, connecting the phrase "Spirit of glory and of God" with Isaiah 11:

> Isaiah said about Jesse's branch that "the Spirit of the Lord will rest on him. . . ." The main difference is that Isaiah used a future tense verb, while in Peter we have a present tense, probably to emphasize that the prophecy uttered in Isaiah has now been fulfilled and that the Spirit that was upon Jesus now also rests on Christians. Believers who suffer are blessed because they are now enjoying God's favor, tasting even now the wonder of the glory to come and experiencing the promised Holy Spirit.[8]

The blessed life, then, is the life endowed with the presence of God. Persecution can only be "good" if God is in it. Peter says that God is present with his people when they suffer persecution.

The nature of blessing is here displayed. Blessing is not an abundance of gifts that God gives. Instead, *blessing is God giving himself.* The blessed life is not the life that is lived in the abundance of good things. The blessed life is the life lived in the very presence of the only one who is rightly called Good. The absence of God is a curse, and the curse leads to death. Conversely, the presence of God is a blessing, and the blessing leads to abundant life — whether that life is being lived eating calamari on a beach or whether

---

7 Schreiner, *1, 2 Peter, Jude,* 221.

8 Schreiner, *1, 2 Peter, Jude,* 222. Schreiner disagrees with Davids, who is quoted above, concerning the exact meaning of this phrase.

that life is lived as a prisoner for Christ in a cargo container in Eritrea. We all undoubtedly prefer the former life of blessing over the latter. However, that preference is no indication of spiritual maturity or biblical fidelity, for Scripture has been teaching for thousands of years that in the presence of God there is fullness of joy. Centuries before Christ arrived on earth, David wrote, "You make known to me the path of life, in your presence there is fullness of joy; at your right hand are pleasures forevermore" (Ps. 16:11 ESV). How much more can we know this reality after the advent, passion, and resurrection of our Lord Jesus Christ! God gives himself to his saints suffering persecution. D. A. Carson sums up the verse this way:

> To participate in "the sufferings of Christ" should bring joy (4:13). "If you are insulted because of the name of Christ, you are blessed" (4:14). The blessing that Peter has in mind is not the suffering itself, nor is it alone the potential for character improvement . . . ; rather, it is the very presence of God: "you are blessed, for the Spirit of glory and of God rests on you" (4:14, citing Isa. 11:2).[9]

Peter's writings help to put our beach scene in proper perspective. The beach and its beauty are not inherently the blessing. The scene might just as well have been enjoyed by sea-faring pirates who stopped at this place to get supplies while planning how to sell young women in the sexual slave trade market. Would it be a blessed scene then? What made the scene a blessing was the presence of God in the midst of his people. Scripture does give ample reason to expect many good gifts from God. Where God is present, there is often an overflow of material wealth. Abraham saw his flocks and herds increase. Jacob's flocks increased too as did the number of his offspring. When God delivered his people from slavery in Egypt, he did so in such a way that the Egyptians handed over their gold and jewels. When Solomon asked for wisdom to rule God's people, he was also given great wealth. All of these so-called blessings were blessings only because they signified God's abundant supply for his people. Without God's presence these same possessions may just as easily have been a curse, robbing the same people of faith in God.

---

9   D. A. Carson, "1 Peter," in *Commentary on the New Testament Use of the Old Testament*, ed. G. K. Beale and D. A. Carson (Grand Rapids: Baker, 2007), 1040b.

Peter, being a fisherman by trade, would likely have enjoyed spending time with us on the beach. But he would have encouraged us to treasure the true blessing — the presence of God with us. He likely wouldn't have ignored the setting sun, but he would have delighted in it rightly — to the glory of God.

And without a doubt Peter would have urged our thoughts upward, above the painted sky, that we might be reminded that our true blessing is being named among those who have received both the good news and the spiritual eyes to see "things into which angels long to look" (1 Peter 1:12). For Peter, believers have been "ransomed from the futile ways inherited from your forefathers, not with perishable things such as silver or gold, but with the precious blood of Christ" (1:18–19). To set his sights any lower than on what is truly precious could lead the believer to mistake the gifts of God for the true blessing. Peter reminds his readers that Christ and the glory of his sacrifice for us is our most precious treasure.

So the beach scene for Peter would likely have been viewed as a foretaste of the table-fellowship of the saints in heaven, where Christ is "at the right hand of God, with angels, authorities, and powers having been subjected to him" (3:22 ESV). Consequently, the blessed life has less to do with the presence of fleshly delights and everything to do with the presence of our faithful God.

So great is this blessing that Peter feels compelled to make sure that Christians are neither confused nor deceived about the path to blessing. Peter draws a proverbial line in the sand on God's blessing: "But let none of you suffer as a murderer or a thief or an evildoer or as a meddler" (4:15 ESV). Interestingly, both in the true sense (v. 14) and in the false sense (v. 15), the pursuit of blessing is assumed to travel through suffering. The Christian must discern whether his suffering is in fact on account of Christ or on account of sin or criminal action.

Not all suffering that Christians undergo attains the blessing about which Peter is speaking. Peter will not countenance a "martyr-complex" mentality,[10] in which Christians are overly sensitive to criticisms commonly faced

---

10   A number of articles and books are now surfacing that take issue with Christians viewing themselves as victims. Typically, this victim-mentality is labeled as a "martyr complex." For one example, see Jason Wiedel, *Persecution Complex: Why American Christians Need to Stop Playing the Victim* (n.p.: Crowdscribed, 2015). A similar thesis animates Candida Moss's

by all people. Also, Peter makes plain that rabble-rousers and revolutionaries who end up in prison for political causes are not necessarily blessed by God. Neither is the blessing an aspect of crime and punishment. The blessing of God's presence comes when the suffering is for righteousness's sake (1 Peter 3:14; see Matt. 5:10–12).

Synthesis of Persecution and God's Presence

This survey of Peter's instruction on persecution has demonstrated that persecution leads to blessing. The blessing is not the persecution itself, but the certainty of God's presence with those persecuted on account of Christ. With this understanding, we can close a loop begun with our chapter on Matthew. There we saw that the presence of Christ provoked persecution against Christ's followers. Now we discover that once the persecution has occurred, it becomes the very thing that comforts the Christ-follower because persecution is an indication that Christ is truly present. In this dynamic, we see just how powerful the presence of Christ still is.

Let me illustrate. The old western TV show *Rawhide* featured the stalwart character of trail boss Gil Favor, who led his men and their cattle across the American West on trail ride after trail ride, encountering seemingly insurmountable obstacles along the way. This classic TV series launched the acting career of Clint Eastwood, who starred in the series as the upstart cowhand Rowdy Yates.

In one episode, "Incident with an Executioner," Gil Favor's crew is bedeviled by the presence of a mysterious rider dressed in black who, apparently, is seeking justice (and revenge) against one of the cowboys. Because of the mere *presence* of this executioner following the crew, everyone in the camp begins to feel both guilty and nervous. What if he is there for them? The presence of this dark rider is more potent than the presence of any other person on the trail because this rider represents both a judge and an executioner. He holds the power of judgment and death. His presence causes men to panic, to flee, to fight, to doubt, and to fear. All of the men tremble because each

---

more scholarly work, *The Myth of Persecution: How Early Christians Invented a Story of Martyrdom* (New York: HarperOne, 2014).

of them knows he is guilty of something — even if his sin is not against this particular executioner. Watch *Rawhide* to see how the episode ends. I mention the episode to demonstrate the *power of presence*. One person literally enslaved an entire crew of cowboys.

A more positive illustration could be made by pointing out how different our lives would look if the governor were to show up at our work or school. What if the president of the United States were to make a stop? Everything from the traffic to the telephones would be put on hold to make way for the presence of this powerful figure. One of the worst traffic jams I've been in was when Highway 10 was shut down near its intersection with the Pacific Coast Highway in Los Angeles. We were told the shutdown happened because Israeli Prime Minister Benjamin Netanyahu was in town. The mere presence of a single political leader affected thousands of Southern California drivers.

Another way to see the power of presence is to think of snakes. (Some of you just shuddered at the thought.) I had a nice hike ruined one evening by the mere presence of a single, slithering rattlesnake. Snakes carry a heaviness, a weightiness that far exceeds any singular sample of the species (in a negative sense). Presidents, kings, and queens have a positive weightiness about them. The weight of presence could be referred to as "glory," which is what the Hebrew word for "glory" means. The glory of the president of the United States is much greater than that of any single person who holds the office. Even people who are his political enemies know instinctively to show reverence in his presence. In England, when the queen enters a room, all must stand, men must bow (at the neck), and women must curtsy.

One would think with all this worked-out etiquette for office-holders that we humans might also have worked out a proper manner in which to respond to the *presence* of Jesus Christ, the Son of God, the king of kings. And yet, the truth is, the presence of Christ is met today — as it was in the first century — with both worship (John 20:28) and sneers (Luke 23:35). The presence of the Son of God begets mocking (Luke 23:36), accusations of insanity (John 10:19–20), imprisonment (Mark 15:6), torture (Matt. 27:26), and death (Mark 15:33–39).

Apparently, there is no consensus on how to behave in Christ's presence. What is clear, however, is that no one is neutral in the presence of Christ. And where is Christ present today? According to the New Testament, Christ is always present with his bride, the church. Repeatedly, the New Testament affirms that Christ is present with his people forever (Matt. 18:20; Matt. 28:20; Acts 9:3–6; Acts 18:10; Heb. 13:5). His presence with his people is nowhere more evident than it is in persecution.

Persecution happens because Christ is present (see Matt. 5:10–12). So, on the one hand, the presence of Christ provokes persecution, while, on the other hand, the persecution it provokes ushers in the blessed status for the persecuted because it is a sure sign that Christ is alive in them. It is the power of Christ's presence that provokes Christian persecution. The presence of Christ is actually the root provocateur of persecution. Thus now (just as in Christ's day) there will be times when his presence causes people to think we are crazy (Mark 3:21), unconcerned (Mark 4:38), or even demonic (Mark 3:22). When the presence of Christ in us provokes people to make insults or false accusations, we are *blessed*. The provocation is not (and must not be) our own offensiveness; it must be none other than Christ himself. When it is Christ in us who provokes others to insult us, we should rejoice and be glad. The turmoil is actually the result of Immanuel, "God with us." Christ causes people to believe, but he also provokes others to persecute. His presence is still powerful.

10

JOHN'S WRITINGS:
"IDOLSPIZING" AND VINDICATION

If the world hates you, know that it has hated me before it hated you.

(John 15:18 ESV)

I love to hate the Dallas Cowboys. When friends ask who my favorite NFL team is, I respond, "The New Orleans Saints and whoever is playing the Cowboys."

My prejudice against the Cowboys goes back decades. Growing up in southwest Louisiana, I had two NFL options: the Houston Oilers (Bum Phillips, Earl Campbell, and "Luv ya blue") or the New Orleans Saints (Archie Manning and brown-bag fans). The Cowboys always beat the Saints and Oilers. Fortunately, I also liked the Pittsburgh Steelers. The Steelers had Terry Bradshaw at quarterback, and he was from the Bayou State, so I had to root for him. In fact, Bradshaw and other members of the great Steelers teams of the 1970s hosted a football camp that I attended in high school. My coach for that camp was Mean Joe Green. In those days, one couldn't be both a Steelers fan and a Cowboys fan, so for the sake of the Oilers, Saints, and Steelers, the Cowboys had to go.

Of course, we must be careful when hating the Cowboys. The Bible condemns gloating over the losses of our enemies (Prov. 24:17; Obad. 12). Without gloating, I love to hate the Dallas Cowboys. I have a prejudice against them that causes me to hope they don't succeed. We all have biases that cause us to either like or dislike others. It's natural — even if it's not honorable. We hate to see certain people prosper. We despise the rich who have an easy life handed to them. We sneer at the naturally beautiful girl who always gets the second glance. We loathe to hear the great athlete talking about his skills. We hate the woman who gets promotion after promotion while we struggle to get a decent raise. Some people think they're so smart, so pretty, so talented that we love to hate them.

We assume the fault is with those we hate. But maybe the fault lies within us. Maybe the problem is ingrained in our hearts from birth. Indeed, maybe the problem is endemic to humanity. A core problem in the human condition is our tendency to *idolspize* others. Here's more on this tendency:

> Do you idolspize? Or, more to the point, whom do you idolspize? Let me explain. It recently became clear to me that modern life has spawned a brand new emotion, that psychological sidewalk-crack between envy and idolatry that we often succeed in jumping over, but once in a while fall right through. That's where we meet them, those of superior beauty, character, talent, and intelligence and, if friends, who are never less than loyal, supportive, generous, and kind. For this we loathe them.[1]

The article by Ann Hornaday from which this quote is taken is brilliant. This term "idolspize" is genius, getting to the heart of a ubiquitous human urge. For Hornaday, the urge grew strong within her when she read through a biographical article of a successful woman whom she held in both high esteem and deep contempt. She noticed as she read through this story that she was both idolizing and despising this woman. In other words, this successful woman was the "Dallas Cowboys" of Hornaday's heart. To idolspize (partly to idolize, partly to despise) is to recognize, on the one hand, that you want to be like this person (or share the success of this team), while, on the other hand, recognizing that you (or your team) fall short of that standard. This idolspizing lives in our hearts. Sometimes, the people we hate most are the ones we wish we could be. I wish, for example, that the Saints would be

---

1 Ann Hornaday, "That Wonderful Woman! Oh, How I Loathe Her!" *The Washington Post*, February 22, 2006, accessed December 19, 2015, http://www.washingtonpost.com/wp -dyn/content/article/2006/02/21/AR2006022101862.html.

"America's team," instead of the Cowboys. We despise those who possess what we ultimately desire.

Instead of respecting and admiring (and even applauding) those who get things right, we allow the acid of envy to corrode our hearts and weaken our sensibilities toward others. As a correction, we must be commanded by God to rejoice with those who rejoice. We must be commanded to esteem others more highly than ourselves. We all have a problem that requires correction by the gospel.

Though Hornaday believes that the problem is new, unfortunately it is not. Since the Fall of Adam and Eve, idolspizing has been an ugly fixture of human nature. We smell the aroma of those who get life right, and we desire it, but, because we fall short of the mark, we begin to covet, then to envy their lives, then to despise those who have excelled us. In biblical terms, all human beings recognize righteousness and know that it is good. We also know that we fail to attain to it, for all have sinned and fall short of the glory of God (Rom. 3:23). So hatred rises toward those we should esteem. When we hate others we ought to admire, we are engaged in idolspizing, a form of self-loathing, that is, hating the fact that someone else is more excellent than we are at life.

Darkness Hating Light

Theologically, this self-loathing is a hatred of falling short of the glory of God. But it's way too hard to admit our faults, so we direct our ire against those who seem to get it right. I hated Roger Staubach when he was in "Captain Comeback" mode, leading the Cowboys to victory in the final minute. (More recently, NFL fans have hated Tom Brady and the New England Patriots; college fans hate Nick Saban and Alabama's Crimson Tide.) The teams and people will change; the root cause remains the same. This hatred — this idolspizing heart — is manifest in different ways throughout the Scriptures. It even manifests itself in the context of persecution in John 15. Listen to Jesus's startling statement:

> If the world hates you, know that it has hated me before it hated you. If
> you were of the world, the world would love you as its own, but because

you are not of the world, but I chose you out of the world, therefore, the world hates you. Remember the word that I said to you: A servant is not greater than his master. If they persecuted me, they will also persecute you. If they kept my word, they will also keep yours. (John 15:18–20 ESV)

According to Jesus, the world despises Christians. By the term "world," he means "people associated with a world system and estranged from God."[2] Superficially, Jesus is saying that the world thinks of Christians the way I think of the Dallas Cowboys — predisposed to dislike. This can be an unsettling thought. Why must the world hate us?

The answer is profound. Those people who live in the world apart from the reality that God has defined for the world are forced to live in a false construct — an imagined world of human origin. According to Oxford scholar Oliver O'Donovan, "When we are warned of 'the world,' we are not meant to think that there is a real alternative to God that we might love in his place. 'The world' in this sense is not the real and good world that God has made, nor any other real world, but a fantasy-world of the sinful imagination."[3] In direct reference to John's Gospel, O'Donovan explains, "The world is the organization and commitment of evil to oppose the good. . . . The conflict in which Jesus engaged and which led to his death was not the conflict of dualist myth between two independent realities, the ultimate principles of good and evil, but a conflict between the true and false forms of the one reality."[4]

If O'Donovan is correct in this assessment, then conflict necessarily follows. The tension between the world and the Christian is not the tension of two teams on an equal playing field (like the Steelers and the Cowboys of the 1970s). It is one team on the playing field with the true rules of life's game, and the other team trying to prop up an elaborately imagined and fatally flawed alternate explanation. The Christian's life with its insistence on God's truth can only burst the bubble of the world's imaginary reality. To live faithfully in obedience to Christ is to simultaneously proclaim the two-edged truth that Christ divides humanity into two camps. One of those

---

2   J. P. Louw and E. A. Nida, *Greek-English Lexicon of the New Testament: Based on Semantic Domains* (New York: United Bible Societies, 1996), 106.

3   Oliver O'Donovan, *Resurrection and Moral Order: An Outline for Evangelical Ethics* (Grand Rapids: Eerdmans, 1994), 227.

4   O'Donovan, *Resurrection*, 94.

camps knows and believes the truth; the other neither believes nor obeys (John 3:36). In his exposition of John 3, D. A. Carson sounds similar to O'Donovan:

> Whatever pretence (and it is *only* pretence) the world might have conjured up to justify its evil before the coming of Christ, it has entirely lost now that this sublime revelation from God himself has come. This revelation simultaneously exposes sin and provides its remedy (a theme further developed in 16:8–11); the world that rejects it hates the exposure (3:19–21) and thus denies any need for a remedy.[5]

To use John's own language, the light shines in the darkness, and the darkness hates the light because of the guilt of its evil deeds.

This hatred is nothing less than a hatred of being exposed. Sin and deception thrive in the darkness; righteousness and truth thrive in the light. Those whose world is built on darkness can live as though everything is all right until someone shines a light into their darkness (see John 1:4–5; 3:20; 8:12; 12:35, 44–50). Jesus, the light of life, has shone God's righteousness into the world. Those who have received him walk as he walked — in the light. And the darkness still hates the light. John paints a clear picture of the enmity between Christ and the world. He makes the matter as plain as the difference between night and day. To look at the matter from this perspective, one sees unmistakably that darkness and light are incompatible — not because the light hates the darkness (John 3:16), but because the darkness hates the light (3:19).

However clear John makes the enmity in his Gospel account, he magnifies the tension exponentially in the last book of the Bible. The book of Revelation has been discussed copiously in both academic studies (on authorship, context, purpose) and in popular treatments of end-times, prophecy, and predictions about the future. Space and focus do not allow for treating any of these topics in this chapter. For our purposes here, it is enough to display the cosmic battle between darkness and light as it's presented by the author of Revelation.

---

5   D. A. Carson, *The Gospel According to John*, The Pillar New Testament Commentary (Grand Rapids: Eerdmans, 1991), 527.

So pronounced is the theme of conflict between the church and the world in Revelation that some have framed the book as an early Christian call to cosmic battle. Paul Middleton, for example, investigates the clashes described in Revelation through the lens of a Jewish war tradition and concludes that first-century believers thought of themselves as soldiers in battle, with each instance of martyrdom serving to advance the cause of victory in the cosmic fight between good and evil, between God and Satan.[6] Without agreeing with the whole of Middleton's thesis, we can say he demonstrates convincingly that conflict, martyrdom, and persecution are the warp and woof of John's apocalypse.

The book of Revelation begins with its writer announcing that he is a fellow participant in the tribulation of the church. He is writing from the context of his own imprisonment because of the word of God and the testimony of Jesus (Rev. 1:9). His imprisonment was served in exile on the island of Patmos in the Aegean Sea.

Throughout the book, John speaks of the persecutions the churches are suffering (2:2–3, 9,13,19; 3:10). In chapter 6, John pulls back the curtains of heaven to allow us readers a view, and the revelation is shocking. The souls of the martyrs are crying out from under the altar (probably language of divine sacrifice). Their cries are righteous, longing for an end to the injustice — an end to the darkness and a vindication of the light. The souls cry out loudly, and their "plea is for the martyrs to be vindicated, for their faith to be acclaimed as not misplaced after all. They want to be acknowledged as right. They call for the court of heaven to rule that their martyrdom was wicked. The holy and true character of the heavenly judge guarantees that this must occur."[7]

The war continues throughout the book because darkness clashes with light. The church is pursued hotly by the dragon in chapter 12. In chapter 14, Revelation pronounces yet another blessing for the persecuted:

Here is a call for the endurance of the saints, those who keep the commandments of God and their faith in Jesus. And I heard a voice from

---

6 Paul Middleton, *Radical Martyrdom and Cosmic Conflict in Early Christianity* (New York: T & T Clark, 2006).

7 K. H. Easley, *Revelation*, Holman New Testament Commentary (Nashville: Broadman & Holman, 1998), 109–10.

heaven saying, "Write this: Blessed are the dead who die in the Lord from now on." "Blessed indeed," says the Spirit, "that they may rest from their labors, for their deeds follow them!" (vv. 12–13 ESV)

This glorious book rises toward its crescendo in chapter 19, where the Hallelujah chorus erupts: "Hallelujah! Salvation and glory and power belong to our God, for his judgments are true and just; for he has judged the great prostitute who corrupted the earth with her immorality, and has avenged on her the blood of his servants" (vv. 1–2 ESV).

So there is indeed a battle between the righteous and the unrighteous, between those walking in the light and those in the darkness. History is pointing toward a day when God will finally settle the matter once for all by vindicating his justice and the saints' righteousness. This promise of triumph and vindication induces the saints to cry, "Amen. Come, Lord Jesus!"

Darkness Longing for Light

John's writings leave little doubt that the world still hates Christ and (thus) his people. Thus far, however, we've chronicled only the despising of the light by the darkness. If idolspizing is an accurate way to describe the dynamic of persecution in John 15, then half of the equation is still unproven. In what way is there any positive idolizing in view? In one sense, Hornaday's language breaks down here because the word "idolspizing" does not appear in the Bible. So we can't say that the world idolizes Christians in the sense that Hornaday was idolizing the successful woman in her story.

What we do see in John 15, however, is a dynamic similar to idolspizing. The Christian possesses what the worldling actually desires: *righteousness*. John does not use the technical term for righteousness often, though he does on occasion (5:30; 7:24; 16:8–10; 17:25). The dynamic he describes concerning the enmity between the church and the world, however, is very much in tune with how the rest of Scripture speaks about righteousness. In his letter to the Romans, Paul says of the world, "Since they did not know the righteousness of God and sought to establish their own, they did not submit to God's righteousness" (10:3 NIV). In the Gospel of John, Jesus likewise admonishes the Jews to stop judging by what seems right in their own eyes and start making proper judgments according to the righteousness of God (7:24).

Later in John, the point becomes more clear. In fact, in the John 15 discourse we have been observing, Jesus continues teaching his followers about the tension between the world and the church. According to Jesus, the disciples will be filled with the Holy Spirit from God (16:8). As a result of God's Spirit dwelling in them, these Christians will walk in the light and simultaneously will offend those of the world walking in darkness. In fact, Christians — because of the Holy Spirit given to them — will convict the world concerning sin and righteousness. People of the world hate the followers of Christ because "they resent the disciples' status as Jesus' followers, and his spiritual presence in them stirs the world's antagonism toward God and his purposes in Christ."[8] In truth, they both hate and idolize Christ's followers because Christ's followers are righteous before God. And if it's true that it is Christ's followers who are righteous, then they (who do not follow Christ) are the unrighteous, subject to God's judgment.

As we noticed in our study of Peter, so too here in John we see how significant it is that God is present with his people. His presence provokes the persecution against Christ's followers. The presence of a righteous God in the midst of his people is enough to expose the idols of the worldling's heart. As was the case in Cain's heart, so we see here that self-righteousness and God's righteousness are mutually exclusive. One must go.

So what we see is something akin to idolizing after all. The world sets itself up in its own righteousness and works hard to maintain its deception and even to project its righteousness onto others. The world wants righteousness. When the unbelieving world is confronted with true righteousness — in the face of the illusory righteousness that O'Donovan called a fantasy world and Carson termed a pretense — the result is deep conviction of sin and the fear of judgment (16:8–10).

The fear of death and judgment is a primary motivator in the human condition. The world wants to be right and desires an escape from death and judgment. The presence of God with Christ's followers is a direct affront to the world's desire to maintain a righteousness of its own. In that sense,

---

8   Andreas J. Köstenberger, *John*, Baker Exegetical Commentary on the New Testament (Grand Rapids: Baker, 2004), 464.

then, the Christian is modeling exactly what the worldling most desires: a righteousness beyond scrutiny. The world, then, both idolizes and despises the Christian.

While the term "idolspize" is novel, the concept is as old as humanity itself. The dynamic outlined here in John concerning persecution is very much in concert with what we learned from Genesis. There we saw Cain playing the part of the world against Abel, who represented God's righteousness. Cain, seeking to establish a righteousness of his own, became angry at God's insinuation that his self-righteousness was not good enough. Cain, angry with God on account of righteousness, struck and killed his brother Abel. Abel was a true martyr, a witness to God and his righteousness. What John is saying in chapter 15 is that the spirit of Cain remains alive in the world and is still active in persecuting the righteous. Persecution happens in John's writings because God's righteousness is displayed in and through those who believe in Jesus.

Humility and Utility: Two Underlying Themes of Belonging to Christ

According to John, persecution happens against Christ's followers on account of Christ himself. Notice in John 15:19–21 that the persecution is rooted in Christ (on "account of my name" and because "I chose you out of the world"). Two significant themes are rooted in these phrases.

The first theme is the *humility* involved in these statements. "Jesus has chosen them out of the world (see 6:70–71; 15:16; 17:13–19). This election, not their intrinsic merit, is what constitutes the basis for their inclusion in the new messianic community. This should keep the disciples humble as they go into the world as Jesus' emissaries."[9] The humility comes from the reality that all believers were originally where the worldlings are now: in unbelief. The transfer from darkness to light did not come about through an advanced intellect, better life choices, or inheritance of a superior genetic coding. Primarily, the transfer from darkness to light happened by God's gracious choice. Because Christ chose to give himself to his followers, the world must hate them. Christ's followers, however, cannot boast in their

---

9   Köstenberger, *John* , 464.

suffering. God hasn't loved these followers based on any traits or characteristics in them. Instead, he loved them because he is love (1 John 4:8). He graciously works to give people the right to be called children of God (John 1:12–13; 1 John 3:1). The grace of God's love leads his followers to humble obedience. He dwells in their midst, empowering their obedience (3:36), thus humbling them under his care and in the presence of the watching world. The watching world sees the wonder of their love for one another (13:35) and idolspizes them for it.

The second theme is *utility*. Those who have been chosen by God simultaneously become witnesses for him in the carrying out of his mission on earth. In fact, Jesus prays (in John 17) toward this very end. After the discussion of persecution by the world in chapter 15 and empowerment by the Holy Spirit in chapter 16, John portrays Jesus praying (in chapter 17) that the Father would work through his followers so "that the world may believe that you have sent me" (v. 21).

Even in the face of persecution, the humility of God's people is utilized by God for the sake of mission. Indeed, this persecution dynamic serves in the Gospel of John to offer an invitation for all to believe that Jesus has been sent from God. No one needs to perish. All may have eternal life. Toward the end of the Gospel, John sums up his point: "These [things] have been written so that you may believe that Jesus is the Christ, the Son of God; and that believing you may have life in His name" (John 20:31). What John spells out is the cyclical, synergistic dynamic between persecution and witness. Those who receive Christ (who is God's ultimate witness) also necessarily become witnesses for him. Because they are his witnesses (chosen by him out of the world), they become targets for persecution. Suffering persecution faithfully, these followers become witnesses again to their persecutors. Both the persecution and the consequent witness flowing from it have a purpose in God's plan. Thus, Jesus encourages his followers, "In the world you will have tribulation. But take heart; I have overcome the world" (John 16:33 ESV).

Presently, we are living in the time of the Gospel of John, the time when the opportunity still exists for those in the world to receive the witness of Christ and become children of God (1:12–13). But the day looms on the horizon when Christ will return, his eyes aflame with fire (Rev. 19:12), for the purpose of judging in truth and righteousness. The warning has been sounded by John: "Behold, he is coming with the clouds, and every eye will see him, even those who pierced him, and all tribes of the earth will wail on account of him" (Rev. 1:7 ESV). When Christ, the ultimate witness, is called by God to return to earth, the darkness will have no place to hide from the wrath of God's lamb (Rev. 6:16). Until that day, the darkness will hate the light on account of Christ. Christ's followers will be persecuted, but they — like John the Baptist — will bear witness about the light. The light will shine, and the darkness will not overcome it at any time between now and Christ's return.

Final Justice in Revelation

A day is lingering on the horizon that, when it arrives, will bring all opposition against Christ to an end. Revelation assures its readers that darkness and light are presently at odds; that the darkness pressures the light mercilessly at times; that the light will one day finish the job, expelling the darkness forever (22:5). Revelation is a book written to comfort and encourage the persecuted. As noted above, the author wrote the book out of the context of persecution.

Revelation is also a book with a vast array of provocative imagery. The book has captured the imagination of generation after generation of believers. Often, however, the core encouragement of the book is forgotten in a morass of end-times speculation. The aim of the book is to encourage suffering believers to persevere in faith. Surprisingly to some, encouragement comes from remembering that the wrath of God will finally be poured out against all of Christ's enemies.

Consider some of the passages in Revelation that make this case. Notice the disposition of the saints and the actions of God because of those who have persecuted the followers of Jesus:

- And they cried out with a loud voice, saying, "How long, O Lord, holy and true, will You refrain from judging and avenging our blood on those who dwell on the earth?" (Rev. 6:10)
- "We give You thanks, O Lord God, the Almighty, who are and who were, because You have taken Your great power and have begun to reign. And the nations were enraged, and Your wrath came, and the

time came for the dead to be judged, and the time to reward Your bond-servants the prophets and the saints and those who fear Your name, the small and the great, and to destroy those who destroy the earth." (Rev. 11:17–18)

- And I heard the angel in charge of the waters say, "Just are you, O Holy One, who is and who was, for you brought these judgments. For they have shed the blood of saints and prophets, and you have given them blood to drink. It is what they deserve!" And I heard the altar saying, "Yes, Lord God the Almighty, true and just are your judgments!" (Rev. 16:5–7 ESV)

In these verses and several others throughout Revelation, the saints who suffer are glad there is a final reckoning that displays God's justice toward those who persecute and oppress the bride of Christ. God pours out his wrath in perfect measure. If there is any hint of a problem with God in these descriptions, the problem is not God's wrath. It is God's patience. How long will he wait before he puts an end to those who persecute the church? For John and the saints suffering persecution,

God's just judgment does not create moral problems but profoundly settles them. Hell reassures believers that evil loses, God wins, and that as God's people, they win, too. When believers are experiencing the all too real pain of oppression in the current evil age, these truths are not disconcerting but sources of comfort, signposts for hope. Such persecuted Christians can have confidence that though they suffer now, their pain does not have the last word. And their persecutors do not have the last word. The last word belongs to God — the God who is ever present with his people in the midst of the persecution, and the God who is coming to judge his enemies and vindicate his people.[10]

In John's Gospel, there is still the hope of salvation. Persecution leads to witness. The hope of salvation is even on display in the manner in which

---

10   Chris Morgan, "The SBJT Forum," *Southern Baptist Journal of Theology* 18, no. 1 (Spring 2014), accessed December 30, 2015, http://www.sbts.edu/resources/journal-of-theology/sbjt-181-spring-2014/sbjt-forum/.

unbelievers idolspize believers. Yet the hope is fading with each passing day. Though God remains gracious and compassionate, slow to anger, and abounding in steadfast love to a thousand generations of those who love him, he will by no means leave the guilty unpunished forever (see Exod. 34:6–7). A day of coming judgment will bring persecutors to their divine indictment and to the execution of their eternal punishment. This sober reality encourages Christ's suffering saints who cry, "Amen. Come, Lord Jesus!"

PART 3

THE IMPLICATIONS AND
PRACTICAL APPLICATIONS

11

THE PRESENCE OF CHRIST:

THE SOURCE AND COMFORT OF PERSECUTION

And behold, I am with you always, to the end of the age.
(Matt. 28:20 ESV)

T hose who have suffered speak of how significant the presence of Christ became for them in their time of dire need. They don't speak of Christ in merely experiential terms. They speak of the Jesus Christ of the New Testament, born of the Virgin Mary, crucified under Pontius Pilate, buried, and raised again on the third day.

One such testimony comes from Richard Wurmbrand, the founder of Voice of the Martyrs. Wurmbrand spent more than fourteen years in Romanian prisons. After his release, he traveled in Europe and America and was startled to find a lack of biblical faith in many seminaries:

> I have heard that some students of theology learn that the biblical story of creation is not true, nor that of Adam, nor the flood, nor the miracles of Moses. Some are taught that prophecies were written after their fulfillment; that the virgin birth is a myth; likewise the resurrection of Jesus, that His bones have remained somewhere in a grave; that the Epistles are not genuine; and that Revelation is the book of a madman. Otherwise, the Bible is a holy book! (This leaves a holy book in which there are allegedly more lies than in Chinese Communist newspapers.)

That is what some present Western Church leaders learned when they were in seminaries. That is the atmosphere in which they live. Why should they be faithful to a Master about whom such strange things are said?[1]

If, instead, believers pay close attention to Jesus (as revealed in the New Testament), we will find every reason to remain faithful. And we will find that Jesus will remain faithful to his promise to remain present with his people to the end of the age. Wurmbrand experienced the fulfillment of Jesus's promise when he was in prison. Through being tortured, drugged, and kept in solitary confinement, he came close to losing his sanity. He reports that he was not allowed to see a book for years. He forgot how to write the alphabet. Once released, he struggled to learn how to write the letter "D." Through the suffering and the torture, the only constant for him was the presence of Jesus Christ. Jesus keeps his word to his followers and blesses them with his presence.

As we have seen in Matthew 5:10–12 and elsewhere, Jesus is both the comfort in *and* the cause of persecution. Persecution is a negative reaction to the incarnate presence of Jesus Christ.[2] Or in a fuller expression, persecution is *a retaliatory action* against the revelation of the righteousness of God in Christ, which is represented or proclaimed by the faithful followers of Jesus. Christ's righteousness is the righteousness against which the persecutors react. Christ must be displayed if there is true persecution. Not surprisingly, Christ promises his presence to his followers.

In Matthew 6, Jesus teaches his disciples to maintain faith in the face of anxieties because the Father sees and knows them and will supply their needs. Jesus teaches in 10:19–20 that his disciples need not plan ahead what to say when persecution corners them: "Do not be anxious how you are to speak or what you are to say, for what you are to say will be given to you in that hour. For it is not you who speak, but the Spirit of your Father speaking through you" (ESV). The Trinitarian formulation is indicative of the name into which disciples are to be baptized (28:19) and is itself a noteworthy testi-

---

1   Richard Wurmbrand, *Tortured for Christ* (Bartlesville, OK: Living Sacrifice Book Company, 1998), 81–82.

2   Definition taken from Nik Ripken, *The Insanity of Obedience: Walking with Jesus in Tough Places* (Nashville: B & H Publishing Group, 2014), 38.

mony to the identification of God with his people through Christ. Matthew's Gospel highlights this nearness extensively, such as the promise in 18:20 of the presence of Christ among those gathered in his name. Such intimate, divine presence is the final note sounded by the Gospel, where Jesus says, "And behold I myself am with you always even to the end of days" (28:20; translation mine). This emphatic promise from Jesus is all the more astounding when viewed in relation to the name of Jesus in 1:23 — Immanuel, "God with us." So the Christ of God is and always will be present with his followers.

The significance of the presence of Christ is shown in the expectation of persecution throughout Matthew. Persecution always comes about on account of Christ (5:11; 10:18), his name (10:22), or his righteousness (5:10). In addition, Christ says that receiving a disciple equates to receiving Christ when it comes to the matter of rewards (10:40). The presence of Christ is real with and for the disciples. Those who refuse the disciples are culpable before God for their rejection of his kingdom as in 10:14–15, where the judgments on the towns refusing the disciples will be worse than the judgment on Sodom and Gomorrah. So Christ himself is not to be left out of the persecution equation, even though the violence is perpetrated against his followers. Indeed, the blessings of Matthew 5:10 and 5:11 offer present-tense assurances of identification with Christ. In other words, persecution for righteousness's sake affirms that the persecuted are being mistreated because of their participating in Christ. What could be more encouraging for the believer than to know he is representing God and the kingdom of heaven is his?

This blessing for the disciple is made possible as he acts faithfully on the authority of Christ. By faith, the disciple learns the way of Christ, which is the way of righteousness. As the disciple lives by faith, he puts on display the righteousness of the Christ of God. He demonstrates that he believes the promises Christ has made. Obedience to Christ manifests the reality of the living God. Such identification with Christ fuels the occasions of persecution. The cause is Christ. The issue is the righteousness of God displayed in Christ through the faith of his followers.

Though ultimately it is Christ against whom hostilities are mounted, his followers are those who bear the blows — the insults, the slanders, the beatings, and the imprisonments. Their persecution happens because of the presence of the sovereign Lord Jesus Christ with them. As John says, persecution happens because Christ chose them out of the world to be his people

(John 15:18–19). Lest Christ be diminished in our discussion, we must insist that persecution happens *on account of him, on account of his name,* or *on account of his righteousness* (Matt. 5:10–12; John 15:18–25; 1 Peter 4:14). Hence, it is significant to state clearly that *the cause of persecution is Christ,* and, on occasion, the righteousness of Christ will be on display in and through the faith of his followers.

The following example may help to explain the function of righteousness in persecution and demonstrate how understanding this dynamic is practical. Sister Chang, a house church leader from Henan province in China, was arrested by Communist officials and, without a trial, sent to the local women's prison, where she spent the next several months.[3] Was Sister Chang persecuted? Or was she justly imprisoned for violating the rule of law? Using the regnal righteousness model, we would begin by asking questions related to Christ and righteousness (not about the Communist officials' intentions). What was the occasion that sparked the arrest of Sister Chang? Was this occasion related to righteousness? How was her practice of righteousness related to Christ? Was it faith in Christ and her efforts to represent and/or proclaim him that exposed her to the hostile actions against her by the government? If so, we would have a case of persecution. If not, we may simply have a case of "repression of minority and nonconventional religions."[4]

So what was the occasion of Sister Chang's arrest? Sister Chang, as it turns out, was arrested for proclaiming the gospel of Jesus Christ on the steps of the local police station. Many Christians would agree that this is a righteous act, or, at least, that preaching the gospel is consistent with righteousness. Ostensibly, the case appears to be one of persecution. We may, however, wish to interrogate Sister Chang further concerning her motive for evangelizing on the steps of the police station. Though proclaiming the gospel is an action based on righteousness, doing so on the steps of the police station may not be; it could, instead, be an unrighteous way to call attention to oneself, or it could be an act of defiance against legitimate, governmental sanctions. It

---

3   See Paul Hattaway, *Back to Jerusalem: Three Chinese House Church Leaders Share Their Vision to Complete the Great Commission* (Waynesboro, GA: Piquant, 2003), 116, for this story of Sister Chang.

4   Rosalind I. F. Hackett and Mark Silk, "Introduction," in *Religious Persecution as a U.S. Policy Issue,* ed. Rosalind I. J. Hackett, Mark Silk, and Dennis Hoover (Hartford, CT: Center for the Study of Religion in Public Life, 2000), 1.

could simply be foolish! It could even be sinful. In the Sermon on the Mount, Jesus warned his followers to "beware of practicing your righteousness before men *to be noticed by them*; otherwise, you have no reward with your Father who is in heaven" (Matt. 6:1; emphasis mine).

If Sister Chang's motive was to be noticed by the world or other Christians, then the action against her was not an occasion of righteousness. This fact would be further borne out by the reality that the actions against her were for engaging in illegal activity for the purpose of self-aggrandizement. In that case, there would be no persecution against Christ because there would be no display of his righteousness. Self-aggrandizing actions against government authority do not manifest the presence or righteousness of Christ.

If, however, Sister Chang's motive was to please the Lord in her proclaiming Christ, and if her reasoning were that she was seeking to obey God, seeking for his kingdom to come, then the occasion precipitating the action against her was the occasion of righteousness. This fact would be borne out by the clear connection of her action to the Christ of Scripture, as she was seeking to please him by engaging in activities he expects from his followers (Matt. 5:14–15; 9:35–38; 10:27–28; 28:19). If her actions had been forbidden by Christ, then the situation would not be persecution because those actions would be a *mis*representation of Christ. On the other hand, if her actions accorded with the teachings of Christ, she might expect blessing from the Lord. As it turns out, the Lord did bless her efforts to herald the gospel. She was arrested, was thrown into prison, and converted so many women to Christ in the prison that the warden ordered her release.

But let's consider the case further. The individual police officer who arrested Sister Chang might have had no obvious malice against Christ. He might simply have been following orders. Considering the calculations some have made about the number of Christians in China, it is possible the officer himself was a Christian called to follow his captain's orders and arrest the lady disturbing the peace on the steps. If so, would this still be persecution by our definition? On first glance, it may not be since the definition says that persecution is a retaliatory action in response to the revelation of the righteousness of Christ. In fact, the scene pictured this way militates against our whole thesis that persecution consists in the righteousness of the persecuted rather than in the intention of the persecutor. Have we now come to the place where we must acknowledge the intention of the persecutor? Yes and no. While it is true that the definition of persecution speaks of retaliatory actions (obviously referring to the persecutors), it is not the case that this aspect is the controlling force in the paradigm.

The insistence still remains that the primary consideration is not the motive of the arresting officer, but, rather, the functional display of Christ's righteousness. What may help here is a return to our definitions, specifically to the distinction in kinds of persecution. There are basically two kinds of persecution: individual and institutional. There are times when people are part of a systemic alignment against the cause of Christ, where individuals participating could even be ignorant of the larger issues at stake. The arresting officer may not know of his superior's desire to crush Christianity in the province. He may simply be following orders. The point is that there are both individual and institutional powers and structures who oppose Christ. An individual episode of persecution would occur when an individual — on his own authority — lashes out against the faithful follower of Christ. An institutional episode would occur when a local PSB officer orders his subordinate to arrest a Christian street preacher.

We're getting rather technical now. Are such distinctions necessary? To answer, we might recall the Lausanne persecution paper first mentioned back in chapter 1. Recognizing the need to make disciples of all nations and realizing not all governments want to see Christians making disciples, the Lausanne persecution paper asked specifically for better definitions regarding what it means to suffer for Christ's sake. Indeed, the Lausanne persecution paper asks for several clarifications.

First, it calls for further theological reflection so that Christians will know how to respond to persecution. Before responding to persecution, the Christian must first understand whether the suffering is persecution. If the suffering is the result of foolishness instead of righteousness, then one's response ought to be to learn the way of wisdom. If the suffering is the result of pride or arrogance or angry provocation, then that person will need to repent and learn the way of peace. Only if the suffering is occasioned by righteousness — righteousness related to Jesus Christ — can that person rightly be said to suffer persecution in the New Testament sense. The necessary first step is to recognize rightly the occurrence of the behavior.

A second way the Lausanne persecution paper indicates the need for the categories we have established is less intentional. By proving to have difficulty with its own persecution taxonomy, Lausanne demonstrates the need for better biblical categories. In the "Convener's Preface," Patrick Sookhdeo asserts, "Many situations of repression and persecution are to a greater or lesser extent a result of political and legal principles, decisions and actions in the countries concerned. This report is not intended to carry any particular political message."[5]

The truth of the matter is that nearly every episode of persecution is related to "political and legal principles." Almost always, political and legal issues are intertwined with the persecution of Christians. This reality dates back to the writers of the New Testament. According to Hebrews, Christians had their homes plundered and property seized by the government, probably the Roman government.[6] The persecuted Christians would have been caught in a complete web of political and legal principles. Yet the author of Hebrews believed they were persecuted because of Christ.

The Lausanne persecution paper demonstrates just how difficult it is to disentangle Christian persecution from its political and legal associations. In the section of the paper titled "1.2: Factors Contributing to Persecution," the authors cite globalization, religious fundamentalism, nationalism, mistrust, economic disparity, capitalism, postmodernism, and "the West's so-called War on Terror" as factors that presently contribute to the persecution of Christians.[7] Surely, many other factors could be named, such as terrorism (in Indonesia), drug-trafficking (in Colombia), or democracy (in Iran, China). The persecution of Christians is no more clear-cut today than it was in the day when the writer of Hebrews was encouraging Christians to pay closer attention to Christ and his teachings. How does the Christian know whether his suffering is persecution and not merely the outgrowth of globalization, fundamentalism, or terror attacks? The Lausanne paper bemoans its own inability to classify such occurrences, although it does recognize them.

Some of the difficulty the Lausanne writers experience is related to their

---

5   Patrick Sookhdeo, "Convener's Preface," in "Persecuted Church," paper (no. 32) prepared for the Lausanne Committee for World Evangelization, Pattaya, Thailand, October 2004, accessed February 15, 2015, http://www.lausanne.org/wp-content/uploads/2007/06/LOP32_IG3.pdf.

6   F. F. Bruce, *The Epistle to the Hebrews*, rev. ed., The New International Commentary on the New Testament (Grand Rapids: Eerdmans, 1990), 267.

7   Sookhdeo, "Persecuted Church," section 1.2.

tendency to view *persecution* through the lens of *religious freedom* rather than through the biblical lens of regnal righteousness. This difficulty does not mean that there is no place for studying Christian suffering through categories like religious freedom. Rather, this statement is a recognition of what the Lausanne persecution paper has already noted, namely, that there needs to be a more thorough biblical, theological consideration of persecution. Instead of considering causes of persecution through the framework of Christ-righteousness as recommended in this book, the Lausanne persecution paper considers causes of persecution in relation to sociological factors such as the practice of Islam (including Muslim doctrine, Wahhabism, and anti-West bias); the practice of oriental religions (Hinduism, extremism, nationalism, caste system); the ideology of Communism (Marxism, fear); and the rise of secularism (including freedom of expression, freedom of speech, and church autonomy). As a consequence of following sociological categories, the Lausanne persecution paper labels as causes of Christian persecution what are actually occasions of social and political conflict. Two examples from the Lausanne persecution paper help make this point.

First, in its description of the case of a man named Hammond of the United Kingdom, the Lausanne persecution paper assumes the matter fits under the broad category of persecution, but the discussion of the case takes place solely in the categories of "religious freedom." Hammond, an evangelical Christian who preached regularly in the town square at Bournemouth, was assaulted by thirty or more individuals. The authorities agreed that Hammond was "temperate" in his language and demeanor. Still, Hammond, a 69-year-old in poor health, was beaten. After the incident, he was also arrested and prosecuted for inciting violence (even though the violence he incited was against himself). The reason he was convicted, and the reason the conviction was upheld on appeal after his death, was that the High Court "under section 5 of the Public Order Act 1986 [argued] that 'criticism' of homosexuality as 'immoral' was 'insulting' language and a criminal penalty was appropriate."[8] Considering that Hammond had a sign attached to him that pleaded with people to "Turn to Jesus," the situation was probably a legitimate occasion of persecution.

The occasion of the incident was Hammond's practice of faith in pro-

---

8   Sookhdeo, "Persecuted Church," section 2.4, "Secularism."

claiming Christ in a respectful manner. The cause of his persecution was related specifically to his faith in Christ and his representation of the righteousness of God. However, the Lausanne persecution paper concludes the description with a reflection on the hypocritical nature of religious freedom in the United Kingdom. The paper says of Hammond's case, "Such a 'restricted' form of freedom of expression is of particular concern in the light of the rise of both radical Islam and anti-Semitic discourse. There is a significant undermining of freedom of expression if temperate criticism of Islam or homosexuality receives antagonism and suppression from State and non-State sources, whilst the Christian and Jewish communities face outright hostility."[9] Though true in its assessment of legal hypocrisy, the Lausanne persecution paper fails to consider Hammond's case through the biblical-theological category of persecution.

A second issue that leads to confusion of categories is the Lausanne persecution paper placing the example of Hammond under the heading "Freedom of expression" and including it in a larger section titled "The challenge posed by secularism to the Church in the West." The significance of this title can be seen as it is juxtaposed with the other three titles that make up the four parts of section 2. The other three titles begin with the phrase, "Persecution of Christians." In the discussion of secularism in the West, the Lausanne persecution paper fails to categorize the matter in terms of persecution at all. The discussion of secularism chronicles the loss of a traditional Judeo-Christian freedom of religious expression. The Hammond illustration demonstrates the validity of that conversation, but the whole paper is supposed to be a treatment of persecution against the Christian church. There may be a need for a discussion of the loss of religious freedom, but the main point of the Lausanne persecution paper needs to be focused on Christian persecution. Again, this critique points more than anything else to the need that the Lausanne persecution paper already recognizes—a more thorough biblical-theological consideration of the subject of persecution.

Framing the causes of persecution as the outward actions of individuals or groups against the Christian community, the Lausanne persecution paper ends up defining persecution based on the motivation and action of the persecutor, rather than considering the faithful actions of the persecuted.

---

9   Sookhdeo, "Persecuted Church," section 2.4 (b) (i), "Freedom of Expression."

This approach to defining persecution is not uncommon, but biblically it is not the most helpful approach. First, as was seen most clearly in our study of Peter, Christians are promised reward or blessing if they are persecuted for righteousness's sake. Biblically, then, it follows naturally that Christians will want to understand why they are suffering insults and slanders and beatings and imprisonments. Christians are promised the blessing of Christ if their persecutions stem from his righteousness.

Beyond understanding their own persecution, Christians are also expected to test their own manifestation of righteousness. On the one hand, doing so prevents the Christian from lumping himself into a mass of other victims and possibly falling prey to a helpless victimized status, and, on the other hand, keeps the persecuted Christian focused on overcoming and receiving the promised reward with Christ in heaven. Christians in Pakistan illustrate this point well. Christians in Pakistan are despised by the Muslim majority. Christians make up only 3 percent of the total population of Pakistan. They are offered only the lowest-paying jobs. Following the U.S. invasion of Afghanistan, Christians in Pakistan have become more direct targets of persecution.

According to the Lausanne persecution paper, more than forty Christians were killed and one hundred injured in attacks in Pakistan in 2002. Sociologically, the actions against the Christians can be traced to 9/11 and the military actions of the United States in response.

However, if the Christians think of their suffering in terms of geopolitical events, then their response may be a political one rather than a Christian one. They may feel that they are victims of political associations that they did not choose. They may begin a political movement to distance themselves from the United States, repudiate all that the U.S military is doing, refuse any contact with missionaries from the West, and even refuse aid from the West in an effort to stop the attacks and make clear that they are not associated with the West. The entire situation is focused on and related to political concern. Where is Christ in this? Where is righteousness? Shouldn't the Christian's first response be one of great comfort and encouragement from the Scriptures? He should see how righteousness has identified him with Christ, and he should understand that the kingdom of heaven belongs to such sufferers as he has become. Of course, the suffering may instead cause him to realize that he did not suffer for righteousness because he had not been acting rightly in relation to the Lord. Yet the suffering may sober him and prove his hope in Christ. Either way, he should begin with a Christian, not a political, framework for understanding his suffering so that when he suffers he can, as Peter exhorted, suffer "as a Christian" (1 Peter 4:16).

One may object to this formulation of the persecution dynamic on the basis that persecution is an action taken against another. Just as murder is an action of the perpetrator against the victim, so too persecution is one of a series of actions that the persecutor perpetrates against the persecuted. Thus as we would define the presence of murder by the motives and actions of the murderer, so too we should define the presence of persecution by the motives and actions of the persecutor. While this reasoning is sound enough and surely recognizes that there is moral culpability for those who persecute Christians (even as there are judgments against murderers), still the situation is different with persecution. So different are the situations, in fact, that there are at least three further reasons for not classifying persecution *primarily* by the perpetrator.

First, the actions and motives of persecutors are extremely difficult, if not impossible, to determine. For instance, the Lausanne persecution paper makes repeated references to the War on Terror being a major factor in the increase of persecution of Christians throughout the Middle East and Asia. Can we be sure that Christians suffering in, say, Palestine are suffering more as a result of the War on Terror, or might they be suffering because of retaliation on the part of angry Muslims who have had their houses razed by Israelis? Or their suffering might be a result of political decisions made by the Palestinian Authority on their behalf. Political affiliations and motivations make the actions of governments and individuals perpetrating persecution difficult to classify rightly.

Beyond the problem of political motivations, there is the additional problem of interplay between diverse social and contextual factors. The Lausanne persecution paper, as mentioned above, notes several of these factors: globalization, nationalism, traditionalism, economic disparity. In Marxist countries, for instance, nationalism and economic disparity might always be contributing factors, and everything — even Christianity — is viewed politically. The Lausanne persecution paper notes these contextual realities when it mentions Colombia, where Christians are routinely attacked because they happen to be in the midst of a cross fire between two warring drug cartels, even though they are not directly linked to one side or the other. According to the Lausanne persecution paper, more than one hundred pastors were killed between 1998 and 2004 by these warring factions. Are they casualties of war or persecuted Christians? Their murders do not appear related to the manifestation of the righteousness of Christ, even though they are faithful Christians who die violent, unjust deaths.

Second, even if the motivations and contextual factors were cleared up, the categories would still not be clearly defined because of the deception inherent in the human heart. The teaching of Jesus in the Sermon on the Mount warns the Christian to make sure he seeks first the kingdom of God and the righteousness that inherits the heavenly reward (as opposed to the righteousness of the Pharisees). If those concerned about righteousness might be wrong about their righteousness (the Pharisees), and if those concerned about their righteousness need to examine their motives to make sure they are righteous (the disciples), then how much more is it the case that those who are not concerned about righteousness could be deceived about their own motives! The point has already been made (in the example of Sister Chang) that outward actions may not always disclose inward motives. The truly righteous (according to Jesus's teaching in the Sermon on the Mount) understand this, but even they must have qualifiers such as "for righteousness's sake" because intentions and actions are not always equal — and not always immediately recognizable. The actions and motives of those instigating persecution are, to say the least, difficult to ascertain.

A final reason that defining persecution ought primarily to follow the persecuted and not the persecutor is the possibility that the persecutor is unwilling to recognize his motive in persecuting Christ. The obvious case study here is the apostle Paul, who once persecuted the church of Christ. In persecuting the disciples of Jesus, Paul, according to Acts 9:4–5, was persecuting Christ himself: "Saul, Saul, why are you persecuting *me*?" The passage makes clear that "the persecution of the disciples of Jesus is equivalent to the persecution of Jesus Himself."[10] Paul was persecuting Jesus when he was "breathing threats and murder

---

10 Scott Cunningham, *"Through Many Tribulations": The Theology of Persecution in Luke-Acts*, JSNTSup 142 (Sheffield: Sheffield Academic, 1997), 221.

against the disciples of Jesus."[11] Yet, when Jesus appeared to him on the road to Damascus, Paul asked, "Who are you?" Of course, Paul knew about Jesus and his followers. Paul's presence at the stoning of Stephen is a clear indication of this knowledge. Yet the narratives in Acts 9, 22, and 26 indicate that there was much about Christ that Paul simply did not know. Though Paul knew *about* Jesus of Nazareth, he evidently did not know Jesus until he met him on the Damascus road. Paul was, in fact, persecuting Jesus in a very real sense, but he would not have acknowledged Christ as the object of his persecution at the time.

Definitions of persecution ought primarily to follow the persecuted and ask whether Christians were acting righteously on account of Christ when the negative, hostile reaction took place. There remains a place, however, for considering the actions and motives of the persecutors. On occasion, an instance arises that calls for further consideration.

One such instance occurred when a young baseball player in Kentucky had to forgo playing on a traveling team as a result of his Christian faith. The team had games and practices on Sunday. The Christian player believed his faith demanded that he not miss church services for baseball. As a result of not being with the team on Sunday, he was not allowed to play.

Was this persecution? Most likely not. In this instance, the actions of the alleged persecutor are significant. While it is true that the Christian baseball player was practicing righteousness on account of Christ by attending weekly worship services faithfully (Heb. 10:25), it is also true that the coach had a rule in place long before the Christian joined the team. The rule was simple, reasonable, and measurable. If you miss practice, you will not play.

When believers are faced with difficult decisions such as whether to commit to a traveling team for sports, we are making the same kinds of decisions all families face in a pluralist society. Members of Seventh-Day Adventist churches must decide whether to apply for jobs that require work on Saturday. Muslim truck drivers must decide whether they will transport alcohol in their vehicles. What should an 18-year-old member of the Society of Friends (Quakers) do when he is told that he must register for the draft as a U.S. citizen?

---

11   See Acts 9:1. The passage begs for a thorough discussion of what it means that Jesus is equivalent to his disciples. Is it a question of presence, identification, or mystical union? See Cunningham, *"Through Many Tribulations,"* for a discussion and further reference to the problems of the debate.

In a diverse society such as ours, religious practices will bump into their legal limits frequently. Likewise, the rules of private clubs and organizations (like baseball teams) will challenge our faith. When evangelical Christians struggle to navigate through this maze of rules and regulations, we are doing the same thing Muslims, Jews, Quakers, Roman Catholics, and others are doing. Even if there is the possibility of bias against us, we ought not feel slighted or adopt a victimized mindset. Of all people, we understand patience and longsuffering.

Our understanding of persecution proves intensely practical for navigating life in a fallen world. Putting all of the thoughts of this chapter together, we can hold to a few helpful principles as a result of our study of persecution:

- God in the Spirit through Christ remains present with his people.
- His presence provokes persecution still today.
- The faithful persecuted are blessed on account of him and possess his promised reward.
- We should look for displays of righteousness when trying to define persecution events.
- This means persecution is not primarily defined by the motive of the persecutor.
- We will suffer as a result of living in a fallen world. Persecution is not the same as suffering bias, discrimination, political opposition, or a religious liberty violation.
- We need not adopt a helpless, victimized status.

The conclusion of the matter should be empowerment and encouragement for all believers in Christ. The encouragement of the Beatitudes (and the entire Sermon on the Mount) is for the righteous who are persecuted because of Christ. Explicit in the Sermon on the Mount (and consistent through the New Testament), the disciples of Christ have been given a paradigm for assessing suffering. If believers are identified with Christ on account of their manifesting his righteousness through their faith, then they may count themselves "blessed" in the biblical sense, recognizing their suffering as persecution on account of him.

If, however, they are unable to see the relation between their suffering and Christ's righteousness, then they may conclude that their suffering is not the persecution described in the New Testament. This introspection should also serve as a healthy check on righteousness, to make sure the righteousness believers are displaying is the righteousness of Christ, that is, the Jesus-righteousness that exceeds that of the Pharisees, instead of the self-righteousness of puffed-up religion. Categorizing persecution based on the persecuted seems consonant with the pattern Christ establishes with his disciples in the Sermon on the Mount. The follower of Christ seeks first Christ's kingdom and his righteousness.

12

MINISTRY TO THE PERSECUTED CHURCH: WHY IT SHOULD BE A TOP SOCIAL JUSTICE CONCERN FOR THE CHURCH

> *So then, as we have opportunity, let us do good to ev-*
> *eryone, and especially to those who are of the household*
> *of faith.*
>
> (*Gal. 6:10 ESV*)

Now that we have heard of the plight of Christians from around the world, and now that we have thought through the biblical material concerning why Christians are persecuted, what should we do? How does this information inform our actions?

My guess is that reading through the material has caused something of an emotional roller-coaster ride from grief to anguish to pity. But beyond emotions, we need to act. Studying persecution works against comfort and challenges us to action.

My aim for this chapter is to convince Christians that the most urgent social justice opportunity facing Christians is ministry to the persecuted church. Whatever good Christians are doing in prisons, in homeless shelters, in soup kitchens, in crisis pregnancy centers, and on the streets, we believers have a greater opportunity still to minister to our brothers and sisters in Christ whose suffering is related directly to their faith in Christ. The challenges are great. Our emotions will be obstacles, but they aren't the only ones we face. We face the challenges of our own faith, our own comfort, and our own understanding of what it means to be Christians.

A Burden and Delight

For more than a decade and a half now, I have been engaged on behalf of the church around the world as it undergoes persecution. I have written articles, filmed videos, held conferences, written petitions, gathered food and clothing, and, of course, offered many prayers for my brothers and sisters in Christ. Honestly, this identification with the persecuted church has proved both a burden and a delight.

As a burden, knowledge of the persecuted church has haunted me at times when I might otherwise have been experiencing a joy-filled moment, such as when I've been at the beach with my family and remembered Aasiya Noreen, who because of imprisonment on account of Christ has not been home with her husband or children for more than six years. Such thoughts create a momentary sting, as I am reminded of her discomfort in the face of my own luxurious surroundings.

And yet as a delight, knowledge of persecution has caused me to realize that every moment God gives me with my family or my church is a tremendous blessing that ought not to be squandered. Instead of leaving me burdened, these thoughts deliver a gentle reminder for me to rejoice always and to make the most of my time because the days are evil (as Paul puts it in Eph. 5:16).

The burden-delight persecution pattern has also aided my understanding and interpretation of the Scriptures. Texts such as Paul's declaration in 2 Timothy 3:12 — that anyone who wants to be holy will also face persecution — leave me dubious about my own desires for godliness because of my relative lack of persecution. When I do face insults or slander, texts like 2 Timothy 3:12 cause me also to question whether or not I have a *persecution complex*, redefining every clash of culture — from Phil Robertson's *Duck Dynasty* fiasco to Macy's alleged war on Christmas — into a neat confirmation of the biblical promise of persecution. It's healthy to be challenged with doubt, but the final word for our own souls comes from God, who is not the author of confusion (1 Cor. 14:33). So the Bible's challenges regarding persecution should ultimately strengthen our faith.

There are great delights derived from reading Scripture through the lens of persecution. Having read and heard many testimonies of the persecuted church clinging to the hope of a sovereign Christ triumphantly lifted up,

I now grasp more clearly what the Lord meant when he told his followers, "The one who endures to the end will be saved" (Matt. 24:32 ESV). I understand better the book of Revelation. I heartily say "Amen!" to what R. C. H. Lenski wrote about this book decades ago:

> Revelation is soteriological but at the same time eschatological and telic. From its beginning to its end it is focused upon the end. This end is the eternal triumph of the kingdom, the foe being eliminated forever. Revelation is the book of hope and stimulates the longing of hope. It is the answer to the cry: "How long, O Lord!"[1]

The cry Lenski mentions (and the cry that Revelation answers) was uttered by saints who had been persecuted unto death (Rev. 6:10). The book of Revelation, consequently, offers hope to those needing it in order to persevere through the perilous trials of persecution. It's difficult to imagine how one might fully grasp the significance of Revelation apart from understanding it through the lens of a persecuted church in need of persevering hope.

Having an awareness of persecution, then, has both its benefits and its challenges. Often it is not easy to discern which is the benefit and which is the detriment. Such, I fear, may be the case with my conviction concerning the priority of ministry to the persecuted church. Reading the Scriptures through the lens of persecution has led me to be convinced that social justice — care for the oppressed, the poor, and the needy — begins with those suffering persecution on account of Christ.

This conviction comes from, first, understanding that God himself is the source of all that is good. Thus, he is the standard we use to measure justice. Second, God's nature is to reveal himself — indeed to pledge himself in covenant — to particular people. He makes great promises of protection and provision for these covenant people. And, third, the New Testament reaffirms God's love and care for his own children. The New Testament metaphors for the church reflect this reality. The church is called the family of God, the household of faith, the body of Christ, and the bride of Christ.

---

1 R. C. H. Lenski, *The Interpretation of St. John's Revelation* (Minneapolis: Augsburg, 1943), 23.

Each of these appellations captures an aspect of intimacy shared between God and his people. Each one also binds fellow believers to one another in a similarly intimate bond.

A Family Affair

Consider the implications of the church being called the family of God. If a famine were to break out in the United States and food became so scarce that large numbers of people began dying of starvation, parents would suffer an enormous burden to feed their own children. While it might be heroic for a father to feed all the children in his neighborhood, it would be strange indeed if in doing so he allowed his own children to starve. Such a man would not be heralded as a hero. All would recognize that he should have cared for all kids in the neighborhood, beginning with those of *his own household*. God is Father to his children who have come to him in faith through Christ our brother (Heb. 2:11). Surely he cares deeply for the members of his own household.

Likewise, imagine a wedding scene in which the honorable, expectant groom (Christ) looks down the aisle of history as his bride (the church) makes her way toward the moment of the wedding's conclusion so the two might finally be together forever. As the bride draws closer to the groom, the groom notices others shouting insults at her, defiling her dress, beating her, trying to throw her into prison, and telling her to shut up about her groom and her wedding. Would the groom assume her suffering is the same as the suffering everyone undergoes? Should he not be much more incensed that *his* bride is being targeted by *his* enemies because of *him*? It surely seems so.

The Bible uses intimate language often to make plain how great a love the Father has for his own children. Once we understand that nearness, we will understand also the urgency that the Bible — and especially the New Testament — places on ministry to the persecuted and oppressed people of God. So let's trace the argument for understanding the priority of ministry to the covenant people (church) of God through the three phases mentioned above: God in the Old Testament; covenant community in the Old Testament; and the New Testament church.

Old Testament: God of Justice

Any fair reading of the Old Testament would recognize the concern God has for those who are marginalized, oppressed, suffering, and vulnerable. In a sweeping, yet succinct overview of the Old Testament, Christopher Wright says the following:

> The prophets saw a people whose appetite for worship was insatiable but whose daily lives were a denial of all the moral standards of the God they claimed to worship. There was plenty of charismatic fervor (Amos 5:21–24), plenty of atonement theology in the blood of multiple sacrifices (Isa. 1:10–12), plenty of assurance of salvation in the recitation of sound-bite claims for the temple (Jer. 7:4–11), plenty of religious observance at great festivals and conventions (Isa. 1:13–15). But beneath their noses and under their feet, the poor were uncared for at best and trampled on at worst. Spiritual religion flourished amidst social rottenness. And God hated it.[2]

The Old Testament affirms that God both hates injustice and loves justice. God executes justice on behalf of those who suffer. Nicholas Wolterstorff gets to the heart of the Old Testament's portrayal of God's concern:

> Furthermore, God's love for justice is declared to be an active love: God does justice. "The LORD works vindication and justice for all who are oppressed" we sing when we bless the Lord with the words of Psalm 103 (v. 6). And when we cry for deliverance with the words of Psalm 140 we say, "I know that the LORD maintains the cause of the afflicted, and executes justice for the needy" (v. 12).[3]

Sounding much like Wright and Wolterstorff, Ken Wytsma asserts that the Old Testament demonstrates just how intensely justice matters to God:

---

2   Christopher J. H. Wright, *The Mission of God: Unlocking the Bible's Grand Narrative* (Downers Grove, IL: InterVarsity, 2006), 288.

3   Nicholas Wolterstorff, *Hearing the Call: Liturgy, Justice, Church, and World*, ed. Mark R. Gornik and Gregory Thompson (Grand Rapids: Eerdmans, 2011), 96.

We never worship justice. We worship God. The question is, Can we worship God without justice? Isaiah 58 answers that we can't. One of the most startlingly straightforward chapters in all of Scripture, it opens with God describing His people who claimed to want to know Him: "Day after day they seek me out; they seem eager to know my ways, as if they were a nation that does what is right and has not forsaken the commands of its God. They ask me for just decisions and seem eager for God to come near them. 'Why have we fasted,' they say, 'and you have not seen it? Why have we humbled ourselves, and you have not noticed?'"

God's response spotlighted the contradiction in their lives and indicted them. . . . God then contrasted the Israelites' failed devotion with His true desire for them: "Is not this the kind of fasting I have chosen: to loose the chains of injustice and untie the cords of the yoke, to set the oppressed free and break every yoke? Is it not to share your food with the hungry and to provide the poor wanderer with shelter — when you see the naked, to clothe him, and not to turn away from your own flesh and blood? . . . Empty devotion is a disappointment to God. Justice is a delight."[4]

God clearly reveals himself as one who asks for the kind of devotion that demonstrates love toward the vulnerable and needy. The Old Testament portrays God as one who is just and who thus expects his people to be just. To be *just* means more than being in right relationship to him. It means acting in righteousness toward others — working for justice for all and against injustice. The Old Testament is clear that God has a deep concern for those in need. On this point, there is broad agreement. Yet more needs to be said.

Most scholars agree that any claim for justice ought to take seriously the nature of God. What is not as broadly recognized is how distinctly God's heart for justice is aimed first toward his covenant people. *Justice* in the Old Testament has its center in God, and it seems to move outwardly from God to and through his covenant people, radiating outwardly to the world. Few have articulated this aspect of the Old Testament view of justice more clearly than Christopher Wright. He understands the biblical terms "justice" and

---

4   Ken Wytsma, *Pursuing Justice: The Call to Live and Die for Bigger Things* (Nashville: Thomas Nelson, 2013), 31–33.

"righteousness" to represent a single idea. Wright states, "Possibly the nearest English expression to the double word phrase would be 'social justice.'"[5] The import of pairing the two concepts is highlighted in Wright's assessment of how "social justice" operated as a relationship beginning with God but culminating in the practices of his covenant people. "Thus it is clear," says Wright, "that for Israel the whole idea of justice was wrapped up with the qualities and characteristics of the Lord, their God, and especially connected to the covenant relationship between Israel and the Lord. Justice is essentially relational and covenantal."[6]

Wright's emphasis on relationship begins with the nature of God, but it pushes further to emphasize the covenant relationship God has with his people. Such an emphasis on the theological center working out through the covenantal relations seems to me indicative of the Old Testament expectation of justice and righteousness. For instance, Moses famously asserts, "For the LORD your God is God of gods and Lord of lords, the great, the mighty, and the awesome God, who is not partial and takes no bribe. He executes justice for the fatherless and the widow, and loves the sojourner, giving him food and clothing. Love the sojourner, therefore, for you were sojourners in the land of Egypt" (Deut. 10:17–19 ESV).

In this assertion, Moses clearly claims God as the foundation for the expectation that the Israelites would act justly toward the sojourners in their midst. What must be reiterated from this text, however, is just how radically covenantal it is. God did not indiscriminately deliver people from Egypt as though he had some peevish desire to delimit the population of ancient Egypt. Rather, God delivered this particular people from Egypt so this particular people would be shaped by his holiness and be holy themselves, set apart by his righteousness from the nations surrounding them.

God's actions toward them were expected to shape their actions toward others, especially their actions toward the needy (widows and orphans) in

---

5 Christopher J. H. Wright, *Old Testament Ethics for the People of God* (Downers Grove, IL: InterVarsity, 2004), 257, contra scholars such as Wolterstorff, who insist on a sharp distinction between the terms. See Wolterstorff, *Hearing the Call*, 401–2. Wright clarifies further the use of social justice in light of research provided by John Goldingay, "Justice and Salvation for Israel and Canaan," in Wonil Kim et al., *Reading the Hebrew Bible* (Harrisburg, PA: Trinity, 2000), 169–87.

6 Wright, *Old Testament Ethics*, 258–59.

covenant community with them. In addition to executing justice for the widows and orphans in their midst, God's people were also to love the sojourners who came with needs into their community. God was holy, thus, they were to be holy in relation to one another and to the world. They were first to be a holy nation, a chosen people. All of Deuteronomy 10 is radically oriented around God's relationship to his covenant community (especially vv. 4 and 12).

Many of those writing in the field of social justice have recognized the nature of God (just) and the consequent concern God has for justice related to the poor and vulnerable. Ken Wytsma, for instance, argues for the principle of *extension* in his explanation of why God's people ought to pursue justice. Briefly stated, Wytsma's extension places God so near to the suffering that to neglect the needy is to neglect God and to serve a poor widow is to serve God. "This is the principle of extension: that God takes our actions personally when it affects His possessions and purposes. It's as if we are acting toward Him."[7] For Wytsma, all people are God's possession.

Wytsma's concept of extension is helpful for capturing the significance the Old Testament places on caring for the needy and the vulnerable with whom we share relationships. However, Wytsma doesn't carry out this idea thoroughly enough. For instance, when reviewing Isaiah 58, he fails to capitalize on the significance of not forsaking one's "own flesh and blood." That language is clearly family language. Wytsma does not encourage any preferential care toward relatives or others in the covenant community. His concern does not appear to be with the nearness of the need. Rather, he says "that God has a preferential option for the poor, the orphan, the widow, the alien."[8] Consequently, Wytsma conflates the nearness of relatives and covenant community members with the categories of widows, orphans, and aliens in general.

Wytsma's concept of extension seems right as an indicator of the nature of God and the attachment God has to suffering people. What gets lost, however, is how this concept ought to be applied consistently. Consider, for instance, that Wytsma uses the example of the injury/outrage he would feel if

---

7 Wytsma, *Pursuing Justice*, 171.

8 Wytsma, *Pursuing Justice* , 172. It must be noted that Wytsma distinguishes a preferential care from a preferential love.

someone abducted one of his daughters: "Suppose someone abducted one of my daughters and took her to a faraway place where I could not find her, and then harmed her. My person — my interest, my intention, my love — extends to my daughter, and therefore anyone who harms my child harms me. Anyone who could help my child but chooses not to also harms me. Conversely, anyone who helps my daughter helps me. God feels the same way."[9]

This concept of extension reflects well the Old Testament trajectory of God's concern for righteousness and his consequent anger against unrighteousness. Moreover, this explanation connects well with God's identification with suffering humanity. What is lacking, however, is the recognition of God's covenant faithfulness to his own son, *Israel* (Exod. 4:22–23; 34:6–7). In other words, Wytsma moves from his illustration of outrage at the kidnaping of his *daughter* to the notion that God feels the same way toward *every* person — with no consideration of the significance of God's covenant relation to his own children. Wytsma certainly would be concerned for any father's daughter abducted and sold into slavery, but he admittedly has a particular concern *for his own daughter's* abduction — exactly as it should be. Likewise, while there is a sense in which God has a redemptive concern for all creation — including the people who inhabit it — the larger biblical narrative indicates that he has a unique relationship with and concern for those in covenant relationship with him. God cares deeply for his children. Is this covenant faithfulness not at the heart of both the Old and New Testament presentations of God's purposes for his people?

Wytsma unnecessarily conflates a covenant (particular) paradigm with a civil (universal) paradigm even though his own illustration garners its effect from the emotional impact of particular, familial love. The concept of extension cannot work if it is applied to everyone equally at all times. Such an extension leaves no room to categorize the kidnapped young woman as a daughter. If *daughter* has any meaning, then it must relate back to a particular family member. Such a particular concern is covenantal, not civic. It belongs to a special relationship.

One would not fault Wytsma for "taking personally" an attack against his daughter, and one should not fault God for taking personally an attack against his children. Here in this dynamic is a more robustly consistent

---

9   Wytsma, *Pursuing Justice* , 171.

presentation of the principle of extension. In fact, Wytsma's paradigmatic passage (Isa. 58) emphasizes the familial aspect of God's extension when it says "your own flesh" (v. 7). So Wytsma has picked up on an important point concerning extension, but its application needs to be viewed in terms of covenant relation.

Old Testament Covenant Concern

The Old Testament, then, focuses justice in God and understands that the people called by his name ought also to practice justice, beginning with their own families and their own covenant community. The rationale behind such a design is organic and inescapable. How could an Israelite demand in the name of God that justice be carried out in Samaria or Nineveh or Egypt or Philistia if the Israelite did not first carry out justice in Israel? It was the nation of Israel that was to be a light to the Gentiles. Indeed, Deuteronomy 4:7-8 sums up the thought perfectly: "For what great nation is there that has a god so near to it as the LORD our God is to us, whenever we call upon Him? What great nation is there that has statutes and judgments as righteous as this whole law which I am setting before you today?"

While the concept of covenant community is easily forgotten in conversations regarding civil justice, it ought not be. The watching world should expect to see something different about God's covenant people. Both an individual and a corporate witness was expected to be on display, as each Israelite was shaped ultimately by the just and righteous God, who made them a nation in the first place.

Unfortunately, the Israelites often failed to maintain God's standard of righteousness in their own community. Thus, God sent prophets to proclaim his righteousness, calling the people back to repentance. These prophets and righteous ones often became the persecuted (Jer. 20:2), the outcast (1 Kings 18:4), and the needy (Gen. 37:36). Thus quite often in the Old Testament the righteous and the poor are grouped together. Being righteous was, sadly, often the means by which one became poor. The pairing of these two concepts in Amos 2:6 makes the point: "Thus says the LORD: 'For three transgressions of Israel, and for four, I will not revoke the punishment, because they sell the righteous for silver, and the needy for a pair of sandals'" (ESV).

The shock value of this passage is that it is spoken to the covenant children of Israel. God's people, Israel — of all people in the world — ought to have enacted justice and righteousness. Instead, God's people actually oppressed the righteous. These needy people were not righteous because they were poor; rather, they were poor because they were righteous.[10] Their concern for God's righteousness likely cost them social standing and opportunity, ultimately leading to their being oppressed. God does indeed care for the poor, but he has a particular concern for the righteous poor — which certainly includes the persecuted who are poor on account of him.

New Testament Righteousness

According to Jesus, one of the most grievous aspects of injustice is that it victimizes those who uphold righteousness. Beginning with the murder of Abel by Cain, the righteous have continually been under assault at the hands of the unrighteous. That this is a primary concern of God is made clear by Christ himself when he says,

> Therefore I send you prophets and wise men and scribes, some of whom you will kill and crucify, and some you will flog in your synagogues and persecute from town to town, so that on you may come all the righteous blood shed on earth, from the blood of righteous Abel to the blood of Zechariah the son of Berechiah, whom you murdered between the sanctuary and the altar. Truly, I say to you, all these things will come upon this generation. (Matt. 23:34–36)

The fact that Jesus frames the entire Old Testament in terms of righteousness — and the consequent burden God has to care for the righteous illtreated — informs (or ought to inform) any interpretation of justice mandates in the New Testament.

We saw that the trajectory of *justice* in the Old Testament was an arc that

---

10 This insight was developed in conversation with Jeff Mooney, professor of Old Testament at California Baptist University. He asserts that the righteous often would become poor because of persecution and discrimination against them.

originated with God, moved to his people, and from them reached out to the entire world. The Old Testament pattern is God → covenant community → fallen world.

What does this pattern have to do with the persecuted church and the New Testament's emphasis on caring for those suffering persecution? Consistent with this arc, the flow of justice in the New Testament moves from God to the world through the church. The pivotal crux is the church, which receives righteousness from God, practices it in community, and spreads it to the world.

Ecclesiology, then, is a critical centerpiece for social justice. In Spirit and Word, the church receives the revelation of God's heart for justice and puts it into practice in Christian community. From this covenant community, social justice radiates outwardly to the visitor, the needy, the oppressed, and the vulnerable. The church is a primary means by which God ministers justice to the world. Thus the church is a critical piece in God's accomplishing his purposes on earth. The church, we might say, is Christ's primary earthly concern, and this is true partly because of the church's role of being a minister of justice.

Without viewing the church as the center of the justice dynamic, one could easily miss its significance altogether — particularly in relation to social justice. Nowhere is this tendency to omit the church more clearly displayed than in discussions of "The Great Assize" of Matthew 25, where Jesus gathers the nations and separates them as sheep and goats. Nicholas Wolterstorff agrees with the widely accepted view that Matthew 25 "can be seen as the grand charter of Christian social work."[11] The reason Wolterstorff and others view the passage as a charter for carrying out social justice is that the passage identifies Jesus with the downtrodden. As Wolterstorff puts it, "I find it beyond reasonable doubt that the passage is not about charity but about justice. Jesus is saying that to fail to treat the naked, the hungry, the imprisoned, and so forth with justice is to wrong Jesus himself."[12] Given that the context is the gathering of the nations for final judgment, Wolterstorff's insistence that the text be interpreted in terms of justice appears accurate.

Overall, however, the passage seems to be not so much about *social justice* (as the term is typically understood) as it is about Christ's identification with

---

11 Wolterstorff, *Hearing the Call*, 396. Wolterstorff accepts this appellation only if the passage is understood as one teaching justice, not charity (see pp. 395–402).

12 Wolterstorff, *Hearing the Call*, 396.

his people. Grant Osborne suggests that the two primary themes of the passage are "first the unity of Jesus with his people and then the responsibility of the world to accept and minister to his followers in mission."[13] Osborne's conclusion rests in part on the phrase "the least of these my brothers," which he understands to be a reference to Christians:

> Thus, it refers to the way the nations treat Christ's *elachistoi* ("little ones" in 18:6, 10, 14), those who in the eyes of the world are "least" in importance. In 12:48–50 Jesus' followers are clearly his "brothers and sisters." Moreover, in ch. 10 all believers are part of Christ's mission. So Jesus' message is that the world will be judged on the basis of how it treats those "little people" whom God is sending to it (so also Gray, Carson, France, Hagner, Blomberg, Morris, Keener, Turner).[14]

The evidence to support Osborne's interpretation is indeed strong. First, even though most scholars in the past century have interpreted the phrase to be a reference to all people universally, the evidence from history is easily on the side of understanding the phrase in the more narrowly focused sense advocated by Osborne and the others here noted.[15] In other words, every era of church history except our own has understood Matthew 25:31–42 to be an identification of Christ with his people. The nations are gathered and separated on the basis of righteousness, which is displayed by how they exercised justice (or injustice!) against the followers of Christ.

If one is predisposed to think in terms of the persecuted church, then the conclusion is obvious: Jesus is identifying with his persecuted (righteous) followers who have become poor, naked, thirsty, and imprisoned on account of him. The nations are held accountable for how they responded to the presence and preaching of Christ through the church. Linking the phrase here in Matthew 25 back to Matthew 10:40–42, Stanley Hauerwas concludes, "In like manner, those who give 'a cup of cold water to one of these little ones in the name of a disciple' (10:42) will have

---

13 Grant Osborne, *Matthew*, Zondervan Exegetical Commentary on the New Testament (Grand Rapids: Zondervan, 2010), 930.

14 Osborne, *Matthew*, 937.

15 Sherman W. Gray, *The Least of My Brothers: Matthew 25:31–42, A History of Interpretation* (Atlanta: Scholars, 1989).

their reward."[16] Hauerwas is alluding to the words of Jesus as recorded in Matthew 10:40–42:

> Whoever receives you receives me, and whoever receives me receives him who sent me. The one who receives a prophet because he is a prophet will receive a prophet's reward, and the one who receives a righteous person because he is a righteous person will receive a righteous person's reward. And whoever gives one of these little ones even a cup of cold water because he is a disciple, truly, I say to you, he will by no means lose his reward. (ESV)

Again, "these little ones" is a reference to the followers of Christ. The concept of prophet here probably hearkens back to Jesus's identification of the disciples facing persecution on account of righteousness just as the prophets faced persecution before them (Matt. 5:10–12). Craig Blomberg adds that the term "little ones" in Matthew without exception refers to the disciples, "while 'brothers' in this Gospel (and usually in the New Testament more generally) when not referring to literal, biological siblings, always means spiritual kin (5:22–24, 47; 7:3–5; 12:48–50; 18:15 [2x]), 21, 35; 23:8; 28:10). There may be a theological sense in which all humans are brothers and God's children, though not all are redeemed, but nothing of that appears here or, with this terminology, elsewhere in Matthew."[17]

The notion that Jesus is closely identified with his followers is found throughout the Gospel of Matthew. The so-called Great Commission (28:18–20) pictures Christ commissioning his followers to make disciples of all nations — the very same nations who will someday be brought before him for justice. Then the commission ends with a promise from Christ to his followers that he will be with them always, even to the end of the age. Christ promises that his presence will be with his followers (see 18:20). When Christ judges the world, he does so with reference to how the world treated his followers (10:40–42; 18:5; 25:40). When Christ first began to train his disciples in the way of righteousness, he did so by telling them

---

16 Stanley Hauerwas, *Matthew*, Brazos Theological Commentary on the Bible (Grand Rapids: Brazos, 2006), 111.

17 Craig L. Blomberg, *Matthew*, The New American Commentary (Nashville: Broadman, 1992), 377–78.

that they would be persecuted on account of righteousness and on account of him (5:10–12).

The picture that emerges from Matthew's Gospel is consistent with the trajectory of the Old Testament: that God identifies uniquely with his people. God pledges himself in faithfulness to his people. He abides in the midst of them. Thus they represent him before the world. The world will be judged by its response to Christ (and his followers). As we have seen, Christ warned his followers from the beginning of the potential for hostile reactions against them. Indeed, Jesus taught them that they were the culmination of a long line of persecuted who suffered as the prophets had on account of righteousness.

Further Clarifications

There are a few problems with interpreting Matthew 25 as a generic call to social action. Placing the presence of Christ with the poor (in the universal, civil sense) is to overlook the importance of the church and God's covenant. Scripture does not show that God pledges the blessing of his presence to the poor, the needy, and the widows *as such*. Rather, Scripture demonstrates that God promises his particular presence with his covenant children in their hour of greatest trials — when they are widowed, orphaned, persecuted, or poor.

In the case of widows, for instance, there is no "free presence" of God pledged to widows simply because they are widows. There are at least two ways this clarification is expressed in the New Testament. First, Paul makes a distinction between those who are widows and those who are widows "indeed" (1 Tim. 5:3–13). In the New Testament, then, even in the case of widows within the covenant community, there is no necessary justice (or mercy) obligation placed on the church on the mere basis of a widow being a widow. Widows in the covenant community first ought to be cared for and sustained by their own families so that the church is not excessively burdened. A family who will not provide such sustenance "has denied the faith and is worse than an unbeliever" (1 Tim. 5:8).

Second, the Old Testament also does not teach that the needy — signified by widows and orphans — are offered a privileged place before God on the basis of their need. Rather, it teaches that within the covenant community

God holds a particular concern for those most vulnerable and in need. The idea is like that expressed by a mother I know whose husband was murdered, leaving her with eight children. She never dreamed of giving any of her children away; even though trapped by grinding poverty, she was determined to provide for them all the best she could. A man once asked her if she played favorites, loving and caring for one of her children above the others. She wisely responded, "I love the one best who needs me the most, whichever one is sick or in need." That seems right, and it seems to reflect the reality of God's concentric, relational concern for his people.

There is no default approval before God on the basis of being a widow or orphan. Consider the judgment foretold against the people of God in Isaiah 9:8–21, which includes judgment against the fatherless and the widows. One verse is particularly germane: "Therefore the Lord does not rejoice over their young men, and has no compassion on their fatherless and widows; for everyone is godless and an evildoer, and every mouth speaks folly. For all this his anger has not turned away, and his hand is stretched out still" (v. 17 ESV). Such a statement is an indication that widows and orphans in unrighteousness cannot claim special favor with God on the basis of their being widows or orphans. Rather, such a judgment makes sense in biblical perspective only if there is a prior covenant relationship with the people (in this case Jacob). The corruption of that people had become so complete that it reached even to the neediest, weakest, and generally most humble among the covenant people: the widows and the orphans. There is no default approval offered to the fatherless or the widow.

There is, however, approval for those in covenant fellowship with God. These are the righteous ones to whom belongs the kingdom. Within this covenant fellowship, there are some who are in great need. They are the hungry, the naked, the imprisoned, the strangers. We learn from the New Testament that they are Christ's family rejected by the world, yet loved by him. The world in fact is not worthy of them, while Christ himself is not ashamed to call them his brothers and sisters. Christ's family are the ones who do the will of his Father (Matt. 12:49–50). And when his followers do his will and suffer as a direct result of their obedience, God is with them. The church should remain faithful to them too, which explains why the apostle Paul worked so hard on behalf of the impoverished church in Jerusalem to get financial aid to them from other churches (1 Cor. 16:1–3). The offering Christians receive weekly in their worship services is patterned after Paul's example of taking a collection to help other Christians through their time of suffering.

Once we are reminded of the covenant nature of God's promises to his people, then we are poised to understand better the significance of the persecuted church in the dynamic of God's justice. Think back to our definitions in chapter 1. We learned that there is an indiscriminate kind of suffering (like tragedy) that potentially affects all people. And we also learned that there is the suffering of human frailty that also potentially affects all people. God is concerned for the well-being of all in both these instances.

Like God, we all are concerned too when a tsunami drowns Christians, Muslims, Buddhists, and animists. But we are intensely more concerned when the lost soul is our own kinsman. Even if we could be indifferent toward the tragic plight of an unbeliever in a foreign land, we could not maintain such indifference toward our own flesh and blood. And so it is with God and his children, whom he purchased with his own blood. This sounds very close to Wytsma's doctrine of extension — only governed by covenantal, familial parameters.

Now carry the thought a step further. What if the injustice committed against the child of God by the unbeliever were committed against this child on the basis of her being *God's* child? Would that not be a matter of more intense concern for God, who has promised his followers that not a hair of their heads will perish? "You will be hated by all for my name's sake. But not a hair of your head will perish. By your endurance you will gain your lives" (Luke 21:17–19 ESV).

The New Testament pattern is that God promises to be with his people, never leaving them nor forsaking them, particularly in their hour of greatest need. The presence mentioned in Matthew 25 is, first, the covenant presence of Immanuel, God with his people (Matt. 1:23). It is further the presence of Christ with his people in their greatest trials. Jesus told his followers from the beginning that they would be persecuted on account of him (Matt. 5:10–12). He told them that the righteous were always persecuted by the unrighteous (Matt. 5:10–12; 23:35). But he assured his followers that he would never leave them, that he would always be with them, even to the end of age (Matt. 28:20) — at which time he would bring to full justice the nations who persecuted and rejected them, while rewarding those who provided for them a cup of cold water in his name.

For me, reading the text of Matthew 25 through the lens of the persecuted church has made that section of Scripture fall in a parallel line with several other significant texts that demonstrate that Christ is particularly present with those who suffer ill-treatment, persecution, and oppression for no other reason than that they are identified as belonging to him. The writer of Hebrews also reiterates to a community of persecuted Christians (13:3) that Christ promised to be with them, never leaving them or forsaking them (13:4). In heaven, saints persecuted unto death are crying out before the throne of Christ, "How long?" In response, John the Revelator says that "they were each given a white robe and told to rest a little longer, until the number of their fellow servants and their brothers should be complete, who were to be killed as they themselves had been" (Rev. 6:11 ESV). It is as though history itself were related to the persecution of the saints.

In similar terms, the apostle Paul speaks as though his suffering persecution was somehow related both to Christ and to Christ's church: "Now I rejoice in my sufferings for your sake, and in my flesh I do my share on behalf of His body, which is the church, in filling up what is lacking in Christ's afflictions" (Col. 1:24).

Indeed, the New Testament pictures of Christ and the church all argue for a close, organic relationship, whether it is a familial relationship (father, children, brothers), a corporal relationship (body), or a marital relationship (bride). Christ is pictured in the New Testament as present with his covenant bride — especially when she is under attack. Imagine the intense fury of a father or a husband-to-be if someone brutally attacked the bride on her wedding day — such fury reflects the wrath we would expect from a righteous God whose child (and Christ's bride) is suffering violence while walking the aisle of history toward the day of Christ's return.

No one makes this point more plainly than Luke, who chronicles in detail the first Christian martyrdom after Christ. Stephen is persecuted to death in Acts 7. When Stephen's sermon drew the lines between righteousness and unrighteousness (7:51–52), the mob became incensed and proved his very point about them by persecuting him to death. In this — his hour of greatest need — heaven opened, and Stephen saw plainly Jesus Christ standing at the right hand of God (7:56). Typically, Christ is said to be seated at the right hand of the Father. Here, he stands to receive his faithful witness.

With great respect for Wolterstorff, Wytsma, and the many other Christian scholars who genuinely care for the well-being of disadvantaged people, I believe the clearest New Testament promise of Christ's presence — and thus the clearest mandated action for justice on behalf of those suffering — is with the persecuted body of our Lord. Without perhaps diminishing the love we show toward unbelievers and needy people in society at large, we have a justice obligation to care for those who are hungry, thirsty, naked, and outcast because they belong to Jesus Christ. Perhaps the best way to summarize our obligation is simply to quote the apostle Paul from Galatians 6:10: "So then, while we have opportunity, let us do good to all people, and especially to those who are of the household of the faith" (ESV).

13

YOU CAN MAKE A DIFFERENCE

Therefore, my beloved brothers, be steadfast, immovable,
always abounding in the work of the Lord, knowing that
in the Lord your labor is not in vain.

(1 Cor. 15:58 ESV)

A s the previous chapter demonstrated, Christians are obligated to work for justice on behalf of brothers and sisters facing persecution. Biblically, persecution is a high priority for Christian social action. One outcome of such a ministry to the persecuted church is a faithful witness to the world. In John's Gospel, the mark of the Christian church is love for one another. When Christians sacrifice in order to serve other Christians, they provide a witness to the world that they belong to Christ. As Jesus said, "By this all men will know that you are My disciples, if you have love for one another" (John 13:35). Thus we have even more encouragement to minister to brothers and sisters in need. Not only will we be fulfilling our obligation to commands such as to remember the persecuted (Heb. 13:3), but we also will be witnessing to the world concerning the love of God and his salvation.

Now that we understand our obligation to the church and our opportunity before the world, we need to know what exactly we can do. But we have limited resources, limited time, and limited energy. So how can we serve persecuted Christians? For the remainder of this chapter, I hope to answer that question by offering a series of ideas and suggestions. Many of the ideas are transferrable to any church or context. Other ideas may not work in your church or situation but could still serve to generate different ministries that may work.

The most important ministry might be prayer, something all Christians can do. I have heard many speakers say that prayer is the greatest need and the first request of those who suffer persecution.

The apostle Paul speaks several times about prayer and persecution. In 2 Corinthians 1:8–11, he tells of a time in Asia when his team faced afflictions so awful that he was sure he would die. They had no hope. And yet, they did not die. They were delivered by two means — God and the prayers of other believers. Here is what Paul said about this experience:

> Indeed, we had the sentence of death within ourselves so that we would not trust in ourselves, but in God who raises the dead; who delivered us from so great a peril of death, and will deliver us, He on whom we have set our hope. And He will yet deliver us, you also joining in helping us through your prayers, so that thanks may be given by many persons on our behalf for the favor bestowed on us through the prayers of many. (2 Cor. 1:9–11)

Suffice it to say, Paul would not diminish the significant role of prayer for those who are suffering. Of course, most Christians already understand the need to pray. What may not be as accessible is a trustworthy way to pray for the persecuted. General prayers for "those who suffer" seem inadequate to meet the depth of needs outlined in chapter 2. But there are many ways to make prayers more specific.

- Voice of the Martyrs sponsors a ministry called Prisoner Alert (www .prisoneralert.com). On that site there are biographies of and current information about fifteen Christians around the world who are in prison on account of their faith in Christ. Specific prayer points are often given.
- Follow news and updates from the various sources found in chapter 2. At my blog (www.GregoryCCochran.com), I have a newsfeed for Morningstar News, which publishes reliable stories of persecution around the world. Make a habit of praying for the individual Christians mentioned in the stories.

- Get prayer guides for the persecuted church from sites such as "I Commit to Pray" (www.icommittopray.com). Introduce others to the needs of the persecuted church by including these persecuted brothers and sisters on church prayer lists, in mid-week prayer meetings, and during Sunday morning worship service prayer time.
- Encourage appropriate leaders in your congregation to join the International Day of Prayer (IDOP) for the persecuted church. Your church can get appropriate materials to host a prayer night for the persecuted from Voice of the Martyrs or Open Doors. Typically, annual IDOP events take place in November. Many churches join together for that one night to show unity with Christians around the world.

Other than prayer, Christians can serve those in need through a host of good ministries. Projects are available all over the world. Perhaps you and your church could provide business start-up costs for widows whose husbands were martyred. Or you could buy seed packets to provide suffering Christians with the means to feed themselves through farming (https://visionbeyondborders.org/ministries/seeds/). You might even fund a community redevelopment project through Open Doors International (www.opendoors.org). Open Doors uses donations to fund the redevelopment of Christian villages decimated by persecution. Voice of the Martyrs, Open Doors, and Vision Beyond Borders all have ministries that supply persecuted Christians with Bibles and Christian literature.

In one church, we sponsored a softball league each year. In an effort to play softball to the glory of God, we raised the entry fee slightly. The small increase funded a couple of pastors in the Pastor Support Program, sponsored by Voice of the Martyrs. This program provides enough money to feed for a year a pastor serving in a church facing persecution; it costs less than $500 per year, and the sponsor gets a picture and letter from the pastor who receives the funds.

In the same church, we held a friendly cake bake competition each Father's Day. Men would bake and decorate a cake. People in the congregation could "vote" for their favorites with a monetary contribution. The winner was the father who received the most money. The real winners of course were the persecuted Christians who received blankets, clothing, food, healthcare, Bibles, and other supplies. All monies collected were donated to various persecution ministries. Many creative opportunities abound.

Another approach would be to incorporate knowledge of persecution in your church's education curriculum. Pastor Richard Wurmbrand tells the story of the only time he taught a children's Sunday school class. He took the children to the local zoo, showed them the lions, and asked if they were willing to be eaten by lions for Christ. He wasn't asked to teach again.

Fortunately, there are more temperate approaches available. Voice of the Martyrs sponsors Kids of Courage (www.kidsofcourage.com). This curriculum teaches how children around the world live out their faith in non-Christian contexts. In each study, the children receive a Bible lesson, learn a game that is played by the children in the featured country, and get a recipe for a culturally authentic snack. In this way, the children learn how God is at work around the world. Children are exposed to non-American expressions of Christianity.

For adults, there is a lot of information out there, but not as much help for understanding. As mentioned above, great ministry opportunities do exist. Quite a bit of advocacy work is taking place too, though much more needs to be done. For example, developing curriculum for small-group studies needs help. Hopefully, this book will help equip leaders with the knowledge necessary to produce more study materials for small groups, campus clubs, and Sunday schools.

Finally, Christians can and should raise awareness for their suffering brothers and sisters. People sometimes mock attempts to use social media to raise awareness (calling it "slack-tivism"). However, social media can be a great way to let other believers know about prayer needs of suffering Christians. I often change my profile picture to a meme that reminds me to pray for a Christian in need. Right now, my picture reads, "Pray for Asia Bibi," which reminds me to pray for this woman in prison, as well as serving to remind others to do the same.

Hopefully, the biblical material presented in this book will reorient our thinking about what it means to be Christians. The result of such a reorientation should lead us to empathize with those who are suffering persecution. This empathy develops from our understanding of how closely persecution is tied to Christ and the gospel. We should begin more and more to identify with those persecuted since we ourselves are in a body with them.